FIX MY ANNUITY™

ANNUITY INSIDE SECRETS™

HOW WE HELP RETIREES ADD FIVE TO SIX FIGURES BACK TO THEIR RETIREMENT ACCOUNTS—WITHOUT PENALTIES OR PAIN, JUST GAIN.

MARK STOECKER

FIX MY ANNUITY™

ANNUITY INSIDE SECRETS™

How We Help Retirees Add Five To Six Figures Back To Their Retirement Accounts - Without Penalties or Pain, Just Gain.

Book Design by HMDPublishing.com

On The Mark Money, Inc.
5465 Legacy Drive, Ste. 650
Plano, TX 75024
OnTheMarkMoney.com

January 2026 On The Mark Money

ISBN: 979-8-9945290-0-3

"They don't know what you think they know"

- Ken Roberts

DEDICATION

To my mother, who inspired me to become an entrepreneur. Selfless sacrifices were made and not forgotten.

To my wife, Claudia for her trust in the Lord and a supporting role in our creations.

To my grandparents, with the Americana grit and backbone of a true farmers, who knew what seedtime and harvest meant.

INTRODUCTION

How We Help Retirees Add Five To Six Figures Back To Their Retirement Accounts—Without Penalties or Pain, Just Gain.

I want you to know something right up front—the fact that you've carved out this time to read this tells me everything I need to know about you. It tells me you're the kind of person who takes your retirement seriously. You're not content to just "set it and forget it" and hope for the best.

And here's what else I know about you: you've worked hard your entire life. You've done everything right. You've saved, you've invested, you've made responsible decisions. And yet... something doesn't feel quite right about your retirement accounts, does it?

Have you purchased an annuity over the past ten years and find the performance and benefits a bit underwhelming?

I understand completely. We choose annuities for safety, growth and income. We want growth without losses.

Maybe you've looked at your annuity statement and wondered, "Where did all my gains go?"

Maybe your annuity performance doesn't match up with your expectations, especially in rising markets?

Maybe you've felt frustrated that your advisor never calls with better opportunities.

Maybe you've just had this nagging feeling in your gut that you're not getting the growth you deserve on money you worked so hard to accumulate.

If any of that resonates with you, then you're in exactly the right place. Because what I'm going to share with you has already helped hundreds of retirees just like you improve their retirement account values by amounts that will probably surprise you.

Just in the past year, we've helped:

Sherman, a 72-year-old retired Lockheed Martin employee, recovered $105,000 on his $800,000 account that was slowly eroding in fees and poor performance.

Dr. Van Buren, a 70-year-old emergency room physician who was skeptical after losing $400,000 with another "friend" advisor, added $51,483 to his$531,000 in accounts.

Aaron and Cynthia, a 73-year-old couple of retired real estate brokers who felt like they were "treading water," discover $133,650 in savings on their $607,500 portfolio.

Leslie, a recent widow who inherited her husband's underperforming annuity and was nervous about taking withdrawals, improved her situation by $108,600 on her $975,000 account—and now she can take income confidently.

Melvin and Julie, a 69-year-old couple where Melvin recently retired from refinery management, improve their accounts by $113,683 on their $700,000 in annuities.

And here's what's remarkable: these aren't rare, outlier cases. This is what we do every single week. In fact, 80% of the time, when someone comes to us with a fixed index or variable annuity that's over three years old and has more than $200,000 in cash value, we find a way to improve their situation by at least $10,000... and often $20,000, $30,000, $50,000, or more.

Our record? $136,000 added back to a single client's account.

Now, I know what you might be thinking. You might be thinking, "Mark, this sounds too good to be true. If opportunities like this existed, wouldn't my advisor have already told me about them?"

And that's a completely fair question. It's actually the question I hear most often. And by the end, you're going to understand exactly why your current advisor probably hasn't brought this to your attention—and it has nothing to do with you.

Here's what most people don't know: In 2023, something significant changed in the annuity industry. Several of the largest insurance carriers got together and decided they wanted to compete more aggressively for market share. They realized they could capture business from other carriers by making better offers to clients who already had annuities with competitors.

And so they opened up what we call "replacement rules"—essentially making it easier for retirees to refinance their old, underperforming annuities into new products with better growth potential, lower fees, and immediate bonuses that can add thousands or even tens of thousands of dollars to your account.

Some carriers are now offering bonuses as high as 22.50% on transferred funds—as long as the new annuity is genuinely better for the client and operates in their best interest. Some bonus offer percentages far exceed the 22.50% and I'll cover that in a minute and what to look at closely.

These aren't fly-by-night companies. These are some of the most respected names in the insurance industry. And they're competing for your business right now.

So yes—this is absolutely real, it's completely legal, and it's happening every single day across the country.

Here's what we're going to cover in our time together:

First, I'm going to share my personal story—how I went from being just another advisor who thought he was doing everything right, to discovering why so many annuities quietly become some of the worst-performing products in retirement portfolios. And more importantly, it doesn't have to be that way and what you can do about it.

Second, I'm going to show you exactly what I call the "Fix My Annuity™"—the same system I use with clients every single week to identify whether an annuity is truly serving them well, or whether they're leaving tens of thousands of dollars on the table.

Third, I'm going to walk you through real client stories—real people with real names who have given me permission to share what we discovered in their accounts, why their annuities were underperforming, and what happened when they took action.

And finally, I'm going to show you exactly how this works for you—including what makes an annuity a good candidate for refinancing, what the process looks like, and how you can see results in as little as three weeks.

By the time we're done today, you're going to have complete clarity on whether your current annuity is working as hard for you as it should… or whether there's a better option available that your advisor has never mentioned.

CONTENTS

WHO THIS IS FOR (AND WHO IT'S NOT FOR)

Now, before we dive in, let me be really clear about who this is for and who it's not for. Because I want to make sure we're using your time wisely.

This is for you if:

You're between the ages of 55 and 80, either in retirement or getting close.

You have a fixed index or variable annuity worth at least $200,000 that you've owned for at least three years, Or you're in the process of researching the purchase of an annuity.

You've noticed your annuity performance has been... underwhelming. Maybe it's earning less than you expected. Maybe it's not growing at all. Maybe you're paying fees you didn't know about.

You're the kind of person who believes in being a good steward of your money—someone who wants to make sure every dollar you've worked so hard for is working as hard as it possibly can for you.

This is also for you if:

You're concerned about outliving your money.

You want more growth, more income, or better access to your funds.

You value working with someone who's independent—someone who's not tied to just one company's products.

You're open to getting a second opinion on your current situation.

However, this is probably NOT for you if:

Your fixed index or variable annuity is less than three years old (there are surrender charge considerations we need to work around).

You have less than $200,000 in annuity value (oftentimes the economics just don't make sense for smaller accounts).

You're perfectly happy with your current advisor and your current returns, and you're not looking for anything better.

Or if you're just not open to the possibility that there might be a better way to position your retirement accounts.

Does that sound fair?

Good. Because let me tell you who I've worked with recently—and I think you'll see yourself in these stories.

Sherman Gladstone was a 72-year-old retired Lockheed Martin manufacturing employee. He spent his career building airplanes—he wasn't a financial guy. He had a variable annuity and some mutual funds that had been losing money for years. He was paying high fees, dealing with frequent tax issues, and watching his life savings slowly erode. Sherman was worried. This was supposed to be his "rest of your life never have to work again" money, and it was disappearing.

We helped Sherman recover $105,000. And while Sherman has since passed away, I still work with his children today—helping them manage the legacy he left behind.

Calvin Rayburn was an architect. For 30 years, his career was architecture and exterior landscape design—not finance. He came to me feeling, in his words, "stupid" because he didn't understand why his annuity hadn't made any money in four years. He felt like he'd fallen for a sales pitch, and he was embarrassed about it.

Turns out, it wasn't his fault at all—and I'm going to tell you that story in detail. We were able to add $23,909 back to his $348,000 account.

Dr. Keith Van Buren was a 70-year-old practicing emergency room physician. Smart guy, right? But he'd just lost $400,000 in a private placement investment recommended by an advisor friend—and he hadn't even told his wife yet. Let that sink in... $400,000 lost and he had not disclosed this to his wife. Yikes. He was extremely skeptical when he came to me. He couldn't believe any offer could be legitimate.

We showed Dr. Van Buren complete transparency. We analyzed his accounts, showed him exactly what was going wrong, and presented him with the three best options available in the marketplace. He chose one, and we improved his situation by $51,483 on his $531,000 in accounts.

Aaron and Cynthia Tovinsky were 73-year-old retired real estate brokers. Returns were okay, nothing to get excited about. Aaron said they felt like they were "treading water." Cynthia was concerned about security because she wanted to travel to Europe and visit their children—but she didn't feel comfortable with how their accounts were positioned.

We uncovered large internal fees—over 3%—dragging their returns down, along with redundancy in their portfolio and high volatility. After our analysis, we found $133,650 in savings on their $607,500 portfolio.

Do you see the pattern here?

These aren't Wall Street executives or financial gurus. They're engineers, architects, doctors, real estate brokers, teachers, refinery workers—everyday people who worked hard, saved responsibly, and trusted their advisors to do right by them.

They're people just like you.

And here's what they all have in common: They're between ages 55 and 80. They have fixed index or variable annuities over $200,000. Their annuities are at least three years old. And their accounts have been underperforming for reasons they didn't understand—and that wasn't their fault.

If that describes your situation, then this is absolutely for you. Now let me tell you why you should listen to what I have to say.

I've been a General Agent and Registered Investment Advisor for 34 years. I specialize in retirement planning, investment management, and income planning. I work across 48 states. I hold licenses as both an insurance agent and as an independent registered investment advisor, which means I have access to solutions that most advisors—who only operate on one side or the other—will never even see.

But more importantly, I operate as an independent fiduciary. That means I'm not tied to any one insurance company or investment firm. I don't have a quota to meet. My only job is to find the absolute best solution for you, regardless of which company offers it.

I work with the top 30 insurance carriers out of 70 available on the insurance side, and Charles Schwab—the largest independent custodian—on the investment side, giving me access to hundreds of money managers. If there's a better solution out there for you, I can find it and bring it to you.

And here's my guarantee: If I can't improve your annuity account by at least

$10,000, I won't even move forward. There's no point in going through the process if it's not going to make a meaningful difference for you.

Over the years, we've helped clients save $10,000, $20,000, $30,000, $50,000, $75,000, $100,000, and our record is $136,000 added back to a single client's account.

Don't just take my word for it. Here's what Travis Seitz wrote in his five-star Google review:

"Mark Stoecker—On the Mark Money. The name is perfect. Mark has set me up with steady growth and income for the rest of my retirement, with money left for my family and my heirs. Very nice feeling not to have to work with anybody else managing my funds. Mark is on the money."

And here's Dr. Juan Pasada:

"Grace and I met Mark over five years ago. Mark consolidated our various investment accounts to make them easily accessible upon my retirement. He worked with us to attain a retirement portfolio that suited our needs. I retired in June and I could not be more pleased with Mark's financial advice and support. Mark is always available to discuss and answer questions. He makes the drive from Dallas to Georgetown on a regular basis to meet with us and I find that highly valuable. I enthusiastically recommend Mark Stoecker to anyone who is looking for financial advice who really cares about you and your future."

One more—David U:

"I had a great experience working with Mark. He provided us with the investment portfolio that we needed and was forthright with his advice as a fiduciary and completed the transaction without pressure. I would use him again."

So yes, this is absolutely for you—if you're willing to take a serious look at whether your current annuity is truly serving you well, or whether there's a better option available.

Now, I want to be completely transparent with you about something.

It would be easy for me to stand up here and make this all sound simple and straightforward. "Just refinance your annuity and add tens of thousands of dollars to your account—easy!"

But the truth is, it wasn't always this way for me.

What I'm about to share with you—this system, these strategies, this network of carrier relationships—it took me decades to build. It cost me hundreds of thousands of dollars. It nearly destroyed my business multiple times. And there were moments when I seriously questioned whether I was going to make it.

But I'm going to tell you that story. Because I think it's important for you to understand not just what I do, but why I do it this way... and what it took for me to get here.

Because here's what I want you to understand: You don't have to go through what I went through. That's the whole point.

You know, there's a reason I can show you opportunities your current advisor can't. And it has everything to do with a decision I made 15 years ago that almost cost me everything...

WHY YOU SHOULD LISTEN TO ME

So before I share my story with you, let me give you a bit more context about who I am and why I'm qualified to talk about this.

I've been in the financial services industry for 34 years. That's over three decades of working with retirees and pre-retirees just like you.

But here's what makes my practice different from most advisors you'll meet:

I hold dual licenses. I'm both a General Agent on the insurance side AND an independent Registered Investment Advisor on the investment side. Most advisors operate in just one world or the other. That limited perspective means they can only show you half the solutions that are available.

I'm an independent fiduciary. That means I'm legally obligated to put your interests ahead of my own. I don't work for an insurance company. I don't work for a broker-dealer. I work for you.

I have access to the top 30 insurance carriers of 70 major carriers on the annuity and insurance side, and I work with

Charles Schwab—the largest independent custodian in the country—which gives me access to hundreds of money managers on the investment side.

What does that mean for you? It means if there's a better solution out there, I can find it and bring it to you. I'm not limited to just one company's products or one company's agenda.

I operate in 48 states. My practice is completely virtual, which means I can work with clients anywhere in the country. And over the past several years, that's exactly what I've been doing—helping retirees from coast to coast improve their retirement outcomes.

I've developed three specialized methods over the years:

"Fix My Annuity"—which is what we're focusing on here—our annuity refinancing system.

"Wealth Maximize"—our approach to reducing fees and improving growth in investment portfolios.

And "Retirement Income Secrets"—our strategy for creating reliable, tax-efficient income that lasts as long as you do.

These aren't just catchy names. These are systematic approaches I've refined over decades of working with clients, figuring out what works and what doesn't.

And here's the standard I hold myself to: If I can't improve your situation by at least $10,000, I won't move forward.

That's not just a marketing tagline. That's how I operate. Because I don't believe in making changes just for the sake of making changes. If your current situation is already optimized,

I'll tell you that. But if I can find five figures or more in improvements—and I usually can—then we have something meaningful to talk about.

Over the years, clients have left me 47 five-star Google reviews. That's not because I'm pushy or because I pressure people. In fact, if you read those reviews, you'll see several mention that I completed transactions "without pressure" and that I'm available to answer questions.

It's because when you genuinely help people improve their retirement outcomes—when you add $20,000, $50,000, $100,000 back to their accounts—they're grateful. And they want others to know about it.

I have clients I've worked with for 20 years. In fact, here's what Dale wrote in his review:

"I met Mark close to 20 years ago shortly after retirement. Through the years, I've had a few changes to balance the investments. The most important thing is that the investments have made more than I've withdrawn. So Mark, thanks for choosing wise investments. We were able to live very comfortably and should for several years to come.

Twenty years. That's the kind of relationship I build with my clients. This isn't a one-time transaction where I sell you something and disappear. This is a long-term partnership where I'm in your corner, watching out for your best interests, year after year.

So that's who I am today. That's the practice I've built. That's the level of service I provide.

But here's what I want you to know... It wasn't always this way.

There was a time when I was just another advisor, working within the system, doing what I was told, pushing the products my broker-dealer wanted me to push. I thought I was helping people. I thought I was doing the right thing.

And then I started to see the cracks.

I started to notice that the companies I worked for didn't always have my clients' best interests at heart. I started to realize that the products I was being encouraged to sell weren't always the best solutions available. I started to understand that there was a whole world of better options out there—options my clients deserved to know about—but I was being kept from showing them.

And that realization didn't come easy. In fact, it came at a tremendous cost.

What I'm about to share with you is my personal journey—how I went from being a guy working long hours in the oil fields of Oklahoma with sketchy characters and shady deals... to discovering a system that now helps retirees across the country add tens of thousands of dollars back to their retirement accounts.

But I'm going to be honest with you: The path I took was expensive. It was painful. And it nearly destroyed me.

I lost offices. I laid off staff. I had a seminar where 40 people were confirmed to attend... and zero showed up. Zero.

I spent decades—and hundreds of thousands of dollars—figuring this out so that you don't have to.

And that's why I'm so passionate about what I do today. Because I know what it's like to be stuck in a system that doesn't serve you. I know what it's like to trust the wrong people. And I know what it's like to finally break free and see what's really possible.

So let me take you back to where this all started...

BACKSTORY: WHERE I WAS

I grew up in northern Iowa, right in the center of farm country. And if you know anything about farm country, you know that work ethic isn't something you learn—it's just expected.

From the time I was old enough to work, I worked. Yard maintenance. House painting. Detasseling corn for Pfizer. Any job I could get—Godfather's Pizza, the True Value hardware store, even a security guard at a gypsum mill and an anhydrous ammonia plant. (slightly dangerous) I was way too young for some of that work, but I wasn't afraid of a challenge.

I had an interest in business and finance, but I didn't have a clear path. I just knew I wanted to build something better.

Then in the early 1980s, several union plants in my town shut down on pay disputes.. Hundreds of homes went on the market overnight. It was clear this wasn't the place for growth.

So I moved south to Oklahoma and found work in the oil fields. It wasn't my first choice, but it was stable income.

But the oil field business? Long hours, sketchy people, shady deals. I kept thinking, "I can do better than this."

So I got out. Took a banking job in 1983. Normal hours, professional environment. But after a few reorganizations, I realized my upward mobility was locked out. Again.

I moved to Texas, landed at Bank of America. New place, new state. Same results.

So I made another pivot. In 1991, I became a Farmers Insurance agency owner. Finally—entrepreneurship. I was building something of my own.

And then hailstorms hit. And my carrier decided to close for new business. Not for a month. Not for six months.

For five straight years.

I could service existing accounts but couldn't write new business. That's not a business model.

So in 1995, I became a licensed securities broker. By 2000, I'd fully exited home and auto insurance and went 100% into investments.

THE 3 WALLS: OBSTACLES PREVENTING SUCCESS

But here were the three walls I kept running into—over and over:

Wall #1: I didn't know who to trust in this industry.

Everywhere I turned—oil fields, banking, insurance, investments—people had hidden agendas. They were more interested in what benefited *them* than what was right for the customer.

Wall #2: I thought all advisors and all companies operated basically the same way.

I assumed if you worked for a big-name company, you had access to the best products. I didn't realize most advisors are *captive*—they can only sell products from one company. I thought everyone could show clients the best solutions. I was naive.

Wall #3: I believed the products I was told to sell were genuinely the best available.

When a manager hands you a product and says, "This is what we're promoting," you assume it's because it's best for clients, right? You assume they've done their due diligence.

I was wrong.

THE EPIPHANY: THE "AHA" MOMENT

In 1991, I made the leap. I became a Farmers Insurance agency owner.

And you know what? I had a great little start. Great little agency. I was building something. I was finally in control of my own destiny.

And then... hailstorms hit.

Now, here's the thing about insurance companies after a major catastrophe: they get spooked. And my carrier decided it was in their best interest to close for new business.

Not for a month. Not for six months.

For five straight years.

Five years where I could still service existing accounts—handle all the service work, all the claims, all the phone calls—but I couldn't write any new business. No new clients. No growth. Just service work.

That's not a business strategy I could agree with.

So I made another pivot. In 1995, I became a licensed securities broker. And by the year 2000, I had fully exited the retail home and auto insurance business and forged ahead with investments 100%.

And then came 2001 and 2002. The stock market dropped. Hard.

And here's what really struck me: the reps at my broker-dealer—Hartford at the time—they were pretty nonchalant about the whole thing. Almost dismissive.

Like, "Oh well, markets go up and down, that's just how it is."

And I remember thinking, "Wait a minute. These are people's *life savings* we're talking about. This is their retirement. And we're just... shrugging it off?"

It was hard to tell who was really on the side of the customer.

And even after ten years in the business at that point, I guess I was still naive. I expected all advisors to operate ethically. I expected everyone to put the client first.

But I kept asking myself: Who do I trust? Who do I believe?

There were hidden agendas everywhere. And I'd been told the products I was selling were "best in class"—and they failed. Miserably. Especially in 2002.

It was time to find some answers.

THE REAL EPIPHANY: MR. GLADSTONE

And then I met Mr. Gladstone.

Sherman Gladstone. One late Summer Friday afternoon, I received a call from my brokerage VP asking if I could look into an account and go meet with a client. His account was assigned to me after his previous broker recently had passed away. He was calling because the market was dropping. He was very concerned about the "rest of his life" money from his career at Lockheed Martin. Everything he'd worked for seemed to be dropping.

I made arrangements to meet with him that afternoon. I drove to Fort Worth and knocked on Mr. Gladstone's door. I was a bit surprised by a couple things. The first thing I noticed was the power had been turned off.

You see Mr. Gladstone had just returned from the hospital after his chemo treatment and things were in a bit of disarray.

We opened some blinds to get some light.. I also called one of his children to make sure they were fully aware of the situation. They were very thankful.

Then I got to work.

Come to find out, the broker had passed away, things were out of place and unmanaged, but more than that, the CPA was making mistakes. I had a two-foot stack of papers to sort through.

But as I dug into it, I started to see things. I started to connect dots. And what I realized was this: Sherman was being bled dry by fees, by taxes, by poor product placement. And nobody had been paying attention.

So I did something. I stopped the bleeding. I protected his accounts. And I restarted the growth—but in a completely different way.

And when I added it all up—the savings in fees, the savings in taxes, the improved positioning—it came to $105,000 on his $800,000 account.

One hundred and five thousand dollars. That was the moment. That was my "aha."

I realized: There's a way to do this. There's a way to genuinely help people grow and protect their accounts—but you have to be willing to look beyond what one company tells you. You have to be willing to search for the best solution, not just the convenient one.

And that's when I found a new approach—a way clients could grow their accounts and protect them at the same time.

THE PLAN: GOING INDEPENDENT

So I made a plan.

In 2002, I started searching for the best method to spread the word about what I'd discovered. And that method was seminars. Dinner seminars, educational workshops—places where I could sit down with retirees face-to-face and show them what was possible.

And it worked. Business started to grow.

Fast forward to 2008 and 2009. By this point, business was great. I had three offices in the Dallas-Fort Worth Metroplex. I had staff supporting me. We were helping more and more clients.

I thought I'd finally figured it out. And then...

THE CONFLICT: THE SCARY BRIDGE (TIME, MONEY, NEAR-DESTRUCTION)

The BIG Mortgage fiasco hit.

When the subprime mortgage fiasco hit I thought our fixed insurance industry was just fine, nothing to worry about here.

Now, I'd assumed the fixed insurance industry was stable. I thought, "We're dealing with guaranteed products here. We have strong ratings. This won't affect us." As far as annuities were concerned, we're resilient.

I was wrong.

One day, I get a call from my insurance broker. And he says, "Mark, we have a problem. Multiple insurance carriers have decided to stop accepting new business. One major carrier just flat-out cancelled agent contracts. For good."

He said, "The good news is, there are still two carriers accepting new business. The bad news is, you're at the bottom of the list. Call back in a couple of months."

Déjà vu. All over again.

I had a pipeline of business in process from seminars. Clients ready to move forward. Applications ready to submit. Applications already in process.

And it all shut down.

I remember thinking, "How could this happen? These companies are supposed to carry reserves. They're supposed to have reinsurance. They're supposed to be *stable*."

The ratings companies had lied about the company ratings. Back door deals. These carriers were forced to put up reserves on new business when the markets had already turned south and they just didn't have the long term wherewithal to handle the volatility.

They would rather temporarily close for new business than to put good money on a losing position. Only the biggest players hung tight, but changed their rules for accepting new business.

It became a game of who would take the business and was I on the list to send it? The internal "underwriting" rules for client acceptance became tighter, as if the client was the problem. This was just another filter to restrict business.

The companies that were in dire shape, got bailouts from larger companies, some from the government - smaller than today's bailouts of course, but bailouts nonetheless.

Several brokerages and insurance companies pulled products and agent contracts off the market (we're talking thousands of agent contracts) and returned in process applications and shut down operations.

This left advisors like me in a lurch. This was not part of main street news. You never heard about it. For the producer, there was no Covid (PPP) loan, no stimmie check. There's no bailout, tough luck business owner. Figure it out.

It was an ugly day for my business.

Little to no products to sell. No long list companies to take the new business. And my brokerage put me at the bottom of the list.

Meanwhile, I had just opened three offices with staff to support me. I had dinner seminars all over town—prepaid, confirmed, coming up on the calendar.

And then came Inauguration Day. January 2009. President Obama's inauguration. Could it get worse?

I had a dinner seminar scheduled that night. Nice venue in Fort Worth. Forty people confirmed. Forty reservations.

Zero people showed up. Not one.

I will never forget standing in that empty room, looking at 40 place settings, 40 meals ready to be served... and nobody there.

Not. A. Good. Sign.

The next couple of months were very rough. I cancelled months of prepaid marketing. I held out as long as I could, then I laid off my staff. I closed all three offices. I took everything home to regroup.

And I'll be honest with you: it felt like being hit broadside in a car accident. It was a setback I had caused. And I take responsibility for that.

Yes, the finance industry was the cause for the downward spiral.

But on my end? I had expanded too fast. I had put trust in relationships I maybe should have vetted better.

I had relied on companies that weren't as solid as I thought they were. And I paid a large price for that. Emotionally. Financially.

But I made myself a promise: I will never repeat this again.

With the grace of God above, I powered through it with new focus.

REBUILDING: THE BREAKTHROUGH CONTINUES

So I established new relationships. On both the investment advisor side and the insurance broker side. This time, I went fully independent. No limits. No excuses.

I expected my business plans to prosper. I expected the best for my clients as their guide.

And I continued to fine-tune my practice with outside consultants to improve my processes.

Then, during a client review in 2015, I noticed something odd.

I was looking at one of my client's annuity accounts, comparing the performance to the actual market index it was supposed to be tracking.

And the numbers didn't make sense. It was as if the company's data was flawed.

So I called the company. I had legitimate questions. They gave me no legitimate answers.

In fact, they had *failed to credit my client on the proper gains that were there.*

And there was no recourse. The company just... got away with it. And that's when "Fix My Annuity" was born.

I realized: I can connect these dots. I can see when companies are underperforming—sometimes predictably, intentionally even—to the detriment of the client. I can see when they're not even getting close to their forecasts.

But there was one problem.

Back in 2015, the fixed index annuity industry had some self-imposed internal rules on replacements. And these rules were basically designed to conserve business. Old-line thinking. Carriers protecting their turf.

So I helped clients where I could. But the restrictions were frustrating.

THE ACHIEVEMENT: WHAT CHANGED EVERYTHING

Then came 2023.

And suddenly, a light was shined.

These large carriers got together and decided, "Hey, maybe we can capture more market share by opening up these replacement rules—*if* we can make the offer better."

And they did. They made the offers better. Significantly better.

The new rule was simple: the new company would accept the business up to the bonus limit they were offering. And some were offering bonuses as high as 20%.

But it had to be in the best interest of the client. That was the key.

All of a sudden, we had a whole new operating book of business we could work with. And we were off and running.

The best carriers were doing this. The rest sat on their hands.

And now I could talk about something I knew was in the benefit of the client. I could help them get away from old, bad deals.

This was it. This was what I'd been building toward for 20+ years.

HOW IT CHANGED ME: THE TRANSFORMATION

So how did all of this change me?

It taught me that you can't rely on any one company, any one relationship, any one system to have your best interests at heart.

I learned that true independence—real, genuine independence—is the only way to serve clients with integrity.

I learned that most advisors will never tell you about opportunities that exist outside their own product lineup, not because they're bad people, but because the system they work in doesn't incentivize it.

And I learned that if you're willing to go through the fire—if you're willing to lose offices, lay off staff, sit in an empty seminar room with zero attendees, rebuild from the ground up—you can create something that genuinely changes people's lives.

Today, my practice is resilient to any kind of economy. We're not dependent on one line of business. We're nimble. We can pivot. Even if we face another COVID-like event, we're ready.

We operate virtually in 48 states. And we're serving more clients than we ever have before.

And oftentimes, we're bringing net gains back to clients at the level of $30,000, $50,000, $70,000, $100,000, or more.

That code-cracking I went through? That changed my entire practice, my entire approach, my entire business strategy.

But here's what I want you to understand:

You don't have to go through what I went through.

You don't have to spend decades figuring this out. You don't have to lose staff and close offices and sit in empty seminar rooms. You don't have to pay hundreds of thousands of dollars in tuition to the school of hard knocks.

I've already paid that price. And now you get to benefit from it.

HERE'S THE BIG IDEA

Here's what I discovered through all of this:

Most retirees have no idea that the annuity they bought five, seven, ten years ago—the one their advisor told them was the "best option available"—is quietly underperforming.

Not because they made a bad decision. Not because they're not smart. But because the product landscape has changed. The offers have gotten better. And their advisor has no incentive to tell them.

But there's a way to fix it.

There's a way to take an old, underperforming annuity—one that's been sitting there earning mediocre returns, charging high fees, locking you into riders you don't need—and refinance it into a new annuity with better growth potential, lower fees, and an immediate bonus that can add five figures or more to your account.

It's completely legal. It's happening every day. And 80% of the time, when someone qualifies, we can make it work.

That's what I'm going to show you today. Not in theory. Not in hypotheticals. But with real client stories, real numbers, and real results.

So let me walk you through exactly how this works...

SECRET #1:

WHY WORKING WITH AN INDEPENDENT ADVISOR MEANS GETTING THE BEST PRODUCT AVAILABLE (NOT JUST THE ONE YOUR ADVISOR IS PAID TO PUSH)

So now you understand my journey—how I got here, what it cost me, and why I do things differently.

Then came 2023.

But here's what you're probably wondering: "Okay, Mark, that's a great story. But how does this actually *work*? What exactly are you doing that's different? And more importantly—can this actually work for *me*?"

That's the question I want to answer right now.

Because here's the thing: when I first started helping clients refinance their annuities using this approach, even I was surprised by how consistently it worked. And I was surprised by how simple the process actually is—once you know what you're looking for.

Let me tell you about Dan and Pauline Morton.

This is the couple that really showed me just how powerful this approach could be when everything came together.

ANALOGY: "IT'S KIND OF LIKE..."

But before I tell you their story, let me give you an analogy that'll make this really clear.

Think about refinancing a mortgage.

When interest rates drop, what do you do? You refinance, right? You take your old mortgage with a higher rate, you replace it with a new mortgage at a lower rate, and suddenly you're saving money every single month. Maybe you're saving $200 a month, $500 a month—over the life of the loan, that could be tens of thousands of dollars back in your pocket.

Now, here's the question: Does your current mortgage lender *call you* when rates drop and say, "Hey, rates are lower now—you should refinance and save money"?

No. Of course not. Because if you refinance, they lose your business. They lose the interest you're paying them.

So what do you do? You take it upon yourself to shop around. You go to a different lender—maybe an independent mortgage broker who can show you offers from 20 different banks—and you find the best deal available in the current market.

That's exactly what annuity refinancing is.

Except most people don't even know you *can* refinance an annuity. They think once they buy it, they're stuck with it forever. Or they think moving it would trigger massive penalties or taxes.

And their current advisor certainly isn't going to tell them about better options, because—just like that mortgage lender—if you move your annuity, they lose the ongoing fees they're earning from your account.

But here's what makes this even better than mortgage refinancing:

When you refinance a mortgage, you're just lowering your rate. You're not getting a big bonus check added to your principal.

With annuity refinancing, the new carrier will often give you an immediate bonus—sometimes 10%, sometimes 15%, sometimes as high as 20%—just for moving your business to them.

So not only are you getting better growth potential and lower fees going forward, but you're also getting an immediate injection of capital into your account.

It's kind of like refinancing your mortgage at a lower rate... *and* the new bank hands you a $30,000 check just for switching.

That's the power of what we're doing.

BACKSTORY

DAN AND PAULINE MORTON

So let me tell you about Dan and Pauline.

Dan was 68 years old at the time, a retired Boeing engineer. Smart guy. Analytical. The kind of person who reads the fine print and does his research before making decisions.

Dan and Pauline had purchased a couple of annuities at his retirement about three years prior. They'd done their due diligence. They'd met with their advisor. They'd reviewed the paperwork. Everything seemed solid.

But here's the problem: Three years later, both annuities had absolutely no performance. Zero growth. For three entire years.

Now, do you know what it feels like to watch your retirement account sit there, year after year, with no gains?

It's frustrating, isn't it? You start to wonder, "Did I make a mistake? Is something wrong? Should I have known better?"

That's exactly how Dan and Pauline felt.

THE PROBLEM

But here's what was really going on—and this is what most retirees don't understand:

The annuities they'd purchased were loaded with features they didn't need. Income riders. High-fee options. Allocation strategies that were designed to *limit* growth in exchange for guarantees they were never going to use.

On paper, when they bought them, it all sounded great. "You'll have guaranteed income if you need it!" "You'll have downside protection!" "You'll participate in market gains!"

But in reality? The fees were eating away at any potential growth. The allocation caps were so low that even when the market did well, their accounts barely moved. And the income rider they were paying for? They had no intention of turning it on for at least another 10 years.

They were stuck in products that weren't designed for their actual goals.

And here's the kicker: their advisor had never called. Not once in three years. No annual review. No check-in. No "Hey, let's see if there's a better option for you now."

Because why would he? He was earning his fees whether the accounts grew or not.

THE EPIPHANY

So Dan found me—I think it was through an online search or maybe a referral, I can't remember exactly—but he reached out.

And right away, I could tell: Dan was skeptical.

He said to me on our first call, "Mark, how does this work? This sounds too good to be true."

And I appreciated that. Because it meant he was thinking critically. He wasn't just going to jump at the first thing someone told him.

So I said, "Dan, let me show you exactly how this works. Give me your current annuity statements, let me analyze them, and I'll show you—line by line—what's happening with your accounts and what better options exist in the market right now."

THE PLAN

So Dan sent me his statements. And I did what I always do: I put together a full analysis.

I looked at:

- What fees he was paying (visible and hidden)
- What riders he was carrying that he didn't need
- What his allocation strategy was and how it was performing relative to the actual indices
- What surrender charges were still in place
- What his actual goals were for these accounts

And then I went out to the market—all 30+ carriers I work with—and I found the three best options available at that time that matched Dan's goals.

Not the three options that paid me the highest commission. Not the three options one company was pushing that quarter. The three best options for Dan, period.

THE CONFLICT

But here's where it got interesting.

When I presented the options to Dan, he was stunned.

He said, "Wait—you're telling me I can move this money, get an immediate bonus added to my account, *and* get better growth potential going forward?"

I said, "Yes. That's exactly what I'm telling you."

And he said, "But why didn't my advisor tell me about this?" And that's the question, isn't it?

Why didn't his advisor tell him?

Because his advisor was captive to one or two insurance companies. He didn't have access to the 30+ carriers I work with. He didn't have the independence to shop the market. And he certainly didn't have the incentive to move Dan's account somewhere else and lose the ongoing fees.

But Dan still hesitated.

He said, "Mark, I've been burned before. I don't want to make another mistake."

And I completely understood that. So I said, "Dan, here's what I'm going to do. I'm not going to ask you to move everything at once. Let's start with *one* of your annuities. Let me prove to you that this works. And then, if you're happy with the result, we can talk about the others."

THE ACHIEVEMENT

So Dan agreed. We moved forward with the refinance on his first annuity. And the result? We increased his account by $15,366.

Not over 10 years. Not hypothetically. Immediately. The day the transfer completed, his account had an additional $15,366 in it from the bonus, plus he was now in a better growth strategy going forward.

And do you know what Dan did next?

He immediately introduced me to the rest of Pauline's accounts.

He said, "Mark, if you can do this for one account, let's look at everything else we have."

So we analyzed Pauline's variable annuity and her mutual fund portfolio. And we found even more opportunities.

The replacement on Pauline's accounts increased her account values by an additional $30,888.

Combined, Dan and Pauline had a total net gain of $46,254 on their $439,655 in accounts.

That's more than 10% of their total portfolio value—added back to them in net gains—just by repositioning into better products that were available in the marketplace.

HOW IT CHANGED THEM

And here's what Dan told me after everything was complete. He said:

"Mark, for three years, I felt like we'd made a mistake. I felt like I'd let Pauline down by putting our retirement money into something that wasn't working. And I didn't know what to do about it. I thought we were just... stuck."

"But now," he said, "I finally feel like our money is working *for* us instead of against us."

That's what this is really about.

It's not just about the numbers—although $46,000 is significant. It's about peace of mind. It's about knowing you didn't make a mistake. It's about knowing that someone is actually looking out for your best interest and showing you what's truly available.

So let me ask you:

Have you ever looked at your annuity statement and wondered where all the gains went?

Does it frustrate you that your advisor never calls with better opportunities?

Would an extra $30,000 or $40,000 or $50,000 in your retirement account change things for you?

Do you feel stuck with your annuity and not sure if it's a good fit now? Are you uncertain about what you're even paying in fees?

If you answered yes to any of those questions, then you're exactly the kind of person this can help.

Now, here's what I want you to understand:

Dan wasn't a financial expert. He was an engineer. He understood numbers and logic, but annuities? That wasn't his world.

And yet, within three weeks—from the time he first reached out to me to the time his first account was refinanced—he had an extra $15,366 in his account.

Three weeks.

He didn't have to become an insurance expert. He didn't have to spend months researching carriers and products. He didn't have to navigate the paperwork and the regulations and the surrender schedules.

I did all of that for him.

And that's exactly what I'll do for you.

See, here's what makes this personally attainable for you:

First, I have access to over 30 insurance carriers. Not just the big-name companies you see on TV—but also the rising-star companies that are making the most competitive offers right now to capture market share.

Second, I operate as an independent fiduciary. That means I can bring you the best option from *any* of those 30+ carriers, not just the one or two I'm contractually obligated to sell.

Third, I do all the heavy lifting. You don't need to understand the intricacies of surrender schedules or bonus structures or allocation strategies. That's my job. Your job is to simply provide me with your current statements and tell me what your goals are.

And fourth, I only move forward if I can improve your situation by at least $10,000. If I can't hit that threshold, I'll tell you your current annuity is fine and we won't make a change.

So when I say this is personally attainable for you, here's what I mean:

You don't need decades of experience. You don't need to go through the painful learning curve I went through. You don't need to know which carriers are offering the best deals this month.

You just need to take one step: reach out and let me analyze your current situation.

That's it.

Within three weeks, you could be looking at five figures or more added back to your account—just like Dan and Pauline.

Now, I know what some of you might be thinking right now.

You might be thinking, "Okay, Mark, this sounds great for Dan and Pauline. But my situation is different. My annuity might have been a bad choice from the start. Maybe I should have known better. Maybe I made a mistake."

And if that's what you're thinking... I want to tell you about Calvin. Because Calvin came to me feeling *exactly* the same way.

He felt like he'd been foolish. He felt like he should have seen through the sales pitch. He felt embarrassed that his account had gone nowhere for four straight years.

But here's what I discovered when I analyzed his annuity: It wasn't his fault. Not even a little bit.

And I'm going to show you why...

SECRET #2:

WHY YOUR UNDERPERFORMING ANNUITY ISN'T YOUR FAULT (THE HIDDEN CONFLICTS EVEN SOPHISTICATED INVESTORS NEVER SEE)

Now, before we go any further, I need to address something that I see all the time.

When someone comes to me with an underperforming annuity—an annuity that hasn't grown in years, an annuity that's charging high fees, an annuity that just isn't doing what they thought it would do—do you know what they almost always say to me?

They say, "Mark, I feel stupid. I should have known better. I should have read the fine print more carefully. I should have asked more questions."

And every time I hear that, it breaks my heart. Because here's the truth: It's not your fault.

The underperformance of your annuity has almost nothing to do with the decision you made, and almost everything to do with information you were *never given* in the first place.

Let me tell you about Calvin.

ANALOGY: "IT'S KIND OF LIKE..."

Calvin's story is kind of like this:

Imagine you go to buy a car. And the salesman shows you this beautiful SUV. He tells you it has all-wheel drive, great safety ratings, plenty of cargo space. He's excited. You're excited. It seems perfect for your needs.

So you buy it.

But what the salesman *didn't* tell you is that the SUV has a special "eco mode" that's permanently turned on—and when it's on, the all-wheel drive doesn't actually engage. So you're really just driving a two-wheel drive vehicle. And oh, by the way, there's also a $200-per-month "premium safety package" that auto-renews every year that you didn't know you were paying for.

And here's the kicker: the salesman's bonus was tied to selling you that specific SUV with that specific package.

Now, is it *your fault* that you're driving a two-wheel drive SUV and paying for a package you don't need?

No. You made the best decision you could with the information you were given. The problem is, you weren't given all the information.

That's exactly what happens with annuities.

BACKSTORY & PROBLEM

CALVIN RAYBURN

Calvin Rayburn came to me feeling terrible about himself.

Calvin was an architect. For 30 years, his career was architecture and exterior landscape design. Beautiful work. Creative work. But finance and annuities?

That wasn't his world.

And he came to me saying, "Mark, I just don't understand finance. I feel stupid that I fell for this."

His annuity—an A+ carrier at the top — had made *zero returns* for four straight years. Four years. Not a single dollar of growth.

And he was beating himself up about it. He thought *he* was the problem.

THE EPIPHANY: WHAT I DISCOVERED

So I asked Calvin to send me his statements. And I started digging.

And here's what I found—and this is what Calvin had *no way* of knowing:

First, the annuity he'd been sold had a big income rider attached to it. Now, income riders can be useful—*if* you're planning to turn on income in the near future. But Calvin had no plans to turn on income for at least another 10 years. So he was paying fees for a feature he wasn't going to use.

Second, the allocation choices inside the annuity were terrible. They were tied to indices that had been underperforming for *years*. But here's the thing Calvin couldn't have known: BIG Insurance company also owns the "XYZ" allocation funds. Several of the internal investment options in that annuity were "XYZ" funds. And there's an agenda—whether explicit or implicit—to keep clients using "XYZ" allocations because it benefits the parent company.

Third, the caps on those indices were so low that even when the market did well, Calvin's account barely moved. These were "non-starters"—indices that had been on the lowest-returning performance lists for a long time.

Now, do you think Calvin knew any of this when he bought the annuity?

Do you think his advisor explained that BIG Insurance company owns "XYZ" funds and there might be a conflict of interest in the allocation recommendations?

Do you think his advisor said, "Hey Calvin, this income rider is going to cost you growth, and you're not planning to use it for 10 years, so maybe we should skip it"?

Of course not.

THE CONFLICT & ACHIEVEMENT

So I sat down with Calvin and I explained all of this to him. And I said, "Calvin, there is no way you would have known about these internal product relationships. There's no way you would have known about the allocation conflicts or how the fee structures work. This is not your fault."

And I saw the relief on his face. He said, "So I'm not stupid?"

I said, "No, Calvin. You're not stupid. You were just never given the full picture."

So we refinanced his annuity. We moved him into an accumulation-focused product with no income rider holding him back. We chose indices with better historical performance and higher caps. We kept it simple.

And the result? We added $23,909 back to his $348,000 account.

But more than the money, Calvin finally had peace of mind. He wasn't beating himself up anymore. He understood that the problem wasn't him—it was the system.

So let me ask you:

Have you ever felt like you should have known better about a financial decision?

Have you ever wondered if your advisor was telling you the whole story?

Do you feel you're paying fees inside your annuity that you don't fully understand?

If you answered yes to any of those, I want you to hear this loud and clear:

It's not your fault.

You made the best decision you could with the information you were given. The problem is, there are things happening inside these annuities—hidden agendas, internal fee structures, allocation conflicts—that even sophisticated investors wouldn't know about unless they had decades of industry experience.

That's not on you. That's on a system that doesn't always operate in full transparency.

So why does this happen?

It's not because advisors are bad people. Most aren't. But the system they work in creates conflicts.

Maybe your advisor is captive to one company, so they can only show you that company's products—even if better options exist elsewhere.

Maybe they're incentivized to sell products with certain features that generate higher fees—even if you don't need those features.

Maybe the product itself changed *after* you bought it. Some companies intentionally shift product dynamics to move clients toward newer, more profitable offerings.

Or maybe your advisor simply didn't know. Maybe they believed it was a good product because that's what their company told them.

But here's what I want you to understand: Your underperforming annuity is not a reflection of your intelligence or your decision-making ability.

It's a reflection of incomplete information, misaligned incentives, and a system that doesn't always put your best interest first.

And the good news? We can fix it.

Now, some of you might be thinking, "Okay, Mark. Maybe it wasn't my fault. But I've been disappointed before. I've worked with advisors who let me down. How do I know this time will be different? How do I know *you're* different?"

And that's a completely fair question.

In fact, let me tell you about someone who had that exact same question—and had every reason to be skeptical.

His name was Dr. Van Buren. And when he came to me, he'd just lost $400,000 with an advisor he trusted. He was burned. He was skeptical. And he wasn't sure he could trust *anyone* again.

But here's what happened when I showed him complete transparency and a fundamentally different approach...

SECRET #3:

HOW TO CHOOSE AN ADVISOR WHO WILL LET YOU SEE BEHIND THE CURTAIN (SO YOU CAN FINALLY MAKE DECISIONS WITH CONFIDENCE)

So you understand that it's not your fault. You understand that hidden factors you couldn't have known about are probably affecting your annuity's performance.

But here's the question I hear most often—and it's the most important one:

"Mark, I've been disappointed by advisors before. I've trusted people who let me down. How do I know *this time* will be different? How do I know you're not just another salesperson telling me what I want to hear?"

And if you're thinking that right now, I don't blame you. In fact, I'd be concerned if you *weren't* thinking about it.

Because the reality is, there are a lot of advisors out there who don't operate the way I do. And you've probably met some of them.

So let me tell you about Dr. Keith Van Buren.

Because when Dr. Van Buren came to me, he had *every reason* not to trust another advisor. Ever.

ANALOGY: "IT'S KIND OF LIKE..."

Here's the difference between what Dr. Van Buren had experienced and what I do:

Imagine you walk into a Ford dealership. The salesperson there is friendly, knowledgeable, enthusiastic. But here's the thing: they can only sell you Fords. That's it. Even if a Toyota or a Honda would better fit your needs, they can't

show it to you. They don't have access to it. Their job is to sell you the best *Ford*

available—not the best *car* available.

Now imagine instead you go to an independent car broker—someone who represents *you*, not the dealership. Someone who can walk into any showroom in the country and say, "Let me show you every option available and help you choose the one that genuinely fits your needs best."

That's the difference between a captive advisor and an independent advisor.

The captive advisor—whether they work for an insurance company, a bank, or a broker-dealer—can only show you what their company allows them to sell. Even if they *know* a better option exists somewhere else, their hands are tied.

But an independent advisor? We can show you *everything*. And our only job is to find what's genuinely best for you.

Now, most retirees have never worked with a truly independent advisor. They've only worked with captive advisors who *seemed* independent but weren't.

And that's why so many people have been disappointed.

BACKSTORY & PROBLEM

DR. VAN BUREN

Dr. Keith Van Buren was a 70-year-old practicing emergency room physician. Brilliant guy. Decades of experience making life-and-death decisions under pressure.

But when he came to me, he was carrying something heavy.

He'd just lost $400,000 in a private placement investment. And here's the worst part: it was recommended by a close advisor friend. Someone he trusted.

Someone he'd known for years.

The investment turned out to be fraudulent. And as an accredited investor, Dr. Van Buren was on the hook for the loss.

And he *still hadn't told his wife. Not good.*

So when Dr. Van Buren reached out to me about his underperforming annuities, he had a very high degree of skepticism.

He said to me, "Mark, I don't know if I can believe this offer is legitimate. I've been burned. Badly."

THE EPIPHANY: WHAT MADE IT DIFFERENT

So I didn't try to sell him anything. Instead, I did something most advisors never do:

I showed him complete transparency.

I said, "Dr. Van Buren, here's what I'm going to do. I'm going to give you an independent analysis of your annuity accounts. I'm going to show you exactly what's happening inside them—the good, the bad, and the ugly. And then I'm going to show you the top *three* opportunities available in the marketplace right now that could improve your situation."

"And here's the key," I said. "I'm not tied to any one company. I work with over 30 insurance carriers. I also work with Charles Schwab and have access to hundreds of money managers. If a better solution exists *anywhere*, I can find it and bring it to you."

I explained to him that I operate as a fiduciary—which means I'm legally obligated to put his interests ahead of my own. Not just ethically obligated. *Legally* obligated.

I also told him, "Transparency is my standard operating procedure. Whether it's insurance or investments, I'm going to show you everything. No hidden agendas. No buried fees. No conflicts of interest."

THE CONFLICT & BREAKTHROUGH

So we got on a Zoom call and I walked Dr. Van Buren through his accounts. And here's what I found:

His annuities were underperforming for a combination of reasons. The allocation strategies used something called "blended return allocations"—and these particular blends had severely underperformed during a very volatile market environment.

But here's the kicker: the allocations never pivoted. Even when market conditions changed dramatically, the strategy just kept grinding away with the same underperforming approach.

And on top of that, the choices were *already* underweight compared to other offers available in the market. They'd been historically underperforming even *before* the volatile period hit.

So I showed Dr. Van Buren all of this. Line by line. Number by number. Complete transparency.

And then I showed him three different options—from three different carriers—that could address these issues and give him better growth potential going forward.

I explained the pros and cons of each. I showed him the fee structures. I showed him the historical performance of the indices. I answered every question he had.

And at the end of the call, Dr. Van Buren said something I'll never forget.

He said, "Mark, I finally understand what the difference is. You're not trying to sell me *your* product. You're trying to help me find *my* solution."

THE ACHIEVEMENT

Dr. Van Buren chose one of the three options I presented.

And the result? We improved his accounts by $51,483 on his $531,000.

But more importantly, Dr. Van Buren got something he hadn't had in a long time: confidence that someone was genuinely looking out for his best interest.

So let me ask you:

Have you ever wondered if your advisor is showing you all your options, or just the ones they're allowed to sell?

Would it give you peace of mind to work with someone who can genuinely shop the entire market on your behalf?

Does transparency matter to you—knowing exactly what you're paying in fees and exactly how your money is allocated?

Here's what makes my approach different—and why this time truly is different if you choose to work with me:

I'm independent. I don't work for an insurance company. I don't work for a bank. I work for *you.*

I have access to 30+ insurance carriers on the annuity side, and Charles Schwab with hundreds of money managers on the investment side. If a better solution exists, I can find it.

I operate as a fiduciary. I'm legally required to put your interests first. Not just morally—*legally.*

And I promote transparency every single time. You'll know exactly what you're paying, exactly what you're getting, and exactly why I'm recommending what I'm recommending.

That's not how most advisors operate. And that's why so many people have been disappointed.

But that is how I operate. And that's why clients like Dr. Van Buren—who had every reason to be skeptical—ended up trusting me with their retirement.

So before we move forward, I want to cover the basics of annuities to give a basis for the solutions we prescribe with our clients.

ANNUITIES 101

SECTION 1.

WHAT IS AN ANNUITY?

Annuities can play a significant role when placed properly in a blended retirement portfolio. For the person reading this that might be investigating annuities before the purchase, let it be known the purpose of this book is not to be considered the definitive guide to purchasing annuities. It is, however, my field-tested guide with the experience of thousands of client cases, each with their specific idiosyncrasies and the application of a retirement vehicle called an annuity.

It's important to know your options. There are annuity solutions available right now that were unheard of fifteen years ago. You don't have to be stuck. It's also not your fault. They've made it complicated. We can make it clear.

To start, annuities are a deposit contract. Designed for a retirement payout in their origin form, they have evolved and morphed into hybrid financial vehicles over the years with many different features, financial engineering to compete with market driven investments.

Some annuities can be considered an alternative to bonds in respect to safety of principal and effectiveness for yield.

Annuities can be an attractive alternative to equities for those seeking principal protection and market participation as well as a guaranteed source for lifetime income, to solve that monthly expense component in any budget.

Annuities can be sold using a flexible payment premium approach or a single deposit approach generally.

Annuities come in a variety of term lengths. The offerings between companies are competitive. The marketing can be hard to understand; some with bonuses and some without, some with specific riders and some without.

Different crediting method strategies can confuse some of the best advisors, and if it confuses the advisor, it will confuse the client. My black and white analysis is if I can't understand and explain it, let alone validate the mechanics and performance, I won't use it. There's a large amount of marketing spin and shiny objects out there and we're here to cut through the noise.

Six Common Types of Annuities

Here are the basic common annuity types. This is not the end all list. Single premium immediate payout (SPIA), Fixed Interest annuities, Multi Year Guaranteed Annuities (MYGA), Fixed Index Annuities, Fixed Index Lifetime Income Annuities (FIA) and Variable Annuities (VA).

Then there's three lesser known annuities; Registered Index Linked Annuities (RILA), the Negative Floor Fixed Index Annuity and the more unknown (RIA only) Fee Based Advisor driven Variable Annuity Wrapper variety for low cost fund and ETF portfolio management. This last one I'm 99.99% sure you have never heard of because it operates on a fee basis through an RIA and it is not sold on a commission basis. However, that being said, it is very powerful as an asset management tool.

Here we are focusing on the most common Fixed Index and Variable Annuities.

Here are the common take aways on all varieties:

- **SPIA - Single Premium Immediate Annuity (SPIA)-** For immediate payout income, guaranteed and principal protected. Used to drive an income for life or a specific period of time with the guarantee it will not change. Think lottery ticket or lawsuit as examples of use as well as every day retirement needs.

- **MYGA - Multi-Year Guaranteed Annuity (MYGA).** For the investor wanting a stated fixed interest for a period, 3yr, 4yr, 5 yr... 10 yr., guaranteed and principal protected. This would be a direct competitor to a longer term Certificate of Deposit, or bond or bond funds, with the advantage of tax deferral with the MYGA.

- **Fixed Interest - Fixed Interest Annuity** - If it's not a MYGA, it could be a hybrid, with a floating fixed interest rate or a bonus on the first year and a floating fixed interest for a term, principal protected.

- **Fixed Index - Fixed Index Annuity (FIA)** The most common vehicle being used in the principal guaranteed space. This annuity comes in a variety of term lengths (4 yr. - 14 yr.) and will offer a variety of index allocations and crediting strategies and principal protection.

- **Fixed Index Lifetime Income** - Fixed Index Annuity with a Lifetime Income Rider - These are marketed as a hybrid approach to offer both growth and income with the design emphasis on guaranteed lifetime income payout. Often they can be marketed with up front income base bonuses to be attractive to the consumer. The offering of a bonus does not necessarily make it the best offer. Several factors make the top offers attractive. Here's where knowing who you're working with and being shown all available choices makes a big difference.

- **Variable - Variable Annuity (VA)** - Variable annuities are generally a security instrument used to market mutual funds inside a tax deferred wrapper. Primarily variable annuities are marketing these funds through selling agreements with the fund families. The fee exposure internally can average as much as 4% internally annually, so it is wise to review all alternative options. These funds have direct market participation and no principal protection by design. Riders for lifetime payouts are available. There are low cost approaches available through the RIA only channel that can far outpace any retail variable annuity product.

- **RILA - Registered index linked Annuity (RILA)** - New on the scene. The brokerage sides attempt to tap the market share of the FIA space above. A variable annuity with some buffer limit on losses (rider) using a variety of market exposed allocations, some lower cost. From my reviews, there are other options available with less risk or more performance and lower fees.

- **Negative Floor Fixed Index - Fixed Index Annuity with a Negative Floor option -** higher payout opportunity with some limited loss potential. Still principal guaranteed, just a floating negative floor that could impede gains in the short term. Generally a no fee approach and direct competitor to RILAs as I see it.

- **(RIA Only) Fee Based Variable - Fee Based Variable Annuity** - Fee based RIAs can manage ETF and mutual fund portfolios inside a low cost ($20/mo.) tax deferred wrapper charge. Ideal for comparison with any market driven Variable annuity or straight mutual fund portfolio which would benefit from tax deferral. The fee reduction for an RIA-VA versus a traditional Variable Annuity can be hundreds of thousands to millions in savings on fees over time.

How Guaranteed is my money?

The insurance company offering a SPIAs, fixed annuities, MYGA's and Fixed index annuity products make the representation that the principal is guaranteed. This means you cannot take a market loss exposure. This is a contractual requirement. Companies are required to maintain deposit reserves to protect the premiums deposited by every client based on multiple risk factors.

Beginning in 2026, the reserve maintenance models are changing to the new (VM-22) approach, where it effectively requires reserves for a 100% mass-lapse event. The carrier must maintain reserves that can also respond to movements in interest rates, credit spreads, and market volatility. Riders or charges can reduce your principal, but principal will not be reduced by market losses.

WIth regard to Variable annuity products, well, you're directly invested in the market, and you have far less protection with (PBV) or Principal Based Valuation, and emphasis is based on the guaranteed income component to cover guarantees like guaranteed minimum income benefits or death benefits. You can take on market losses and your account values fluctuate with market exposure like any other investment.

Term Lengths:

Annuities come in a variety of contract term lengths; anywhere from 1yr to 15 yrs or more. For this conversation, we would only ever recommend contracts 10 years or less with good reasons which we will discuss.

Short term versus Long Term - Term length can present some interesting options. From my vantage point, over the past 34 years, most ten year contracts, actuarially speaking, have held the advantage when it comes to crediting offers and potential bonus outcomes in the case of replacements.

Only in the last few years have there been new product entrants on the 5 year annuity chassis that have also offered excellent participation growth strategies and even some with bonuses. As more companies compete for market share among other fixed index annuity companies and the equity markets directly, this can only be a plus for better offers to consumers.

We often use 5 yr. Fixed index annuity products to replace the bond portfolio component in managed portfolios. The principal is guaranteed from market losses, unlike bonds which are exposed to market swings. The Five-Year annuity allows a client to pivot at the end of the short term and reassess all options available. It's important to check growth credit strategies between five or seven years and ten year contracts from the same product line.

In my opinion there is no "best interest" client's advantage to 12, 14, 15 year contracts, that they couldn't find in a ten year term or less.

So, How does this work, How do we work, How do we get paid?

As a representative agency of the companies we represent, anytime there is an introduction of a client to the insurance company in the form of a new annuity application, the agency is paid a commission at issuance of that annuity contract.

This is the distribution model of annuity business in the US, commission based, not fee based. The agency gets paid by the company for the introduction to the client in the form of an application for an annuity product, in exchange, the agency is expected to service that client and the contract for the duration.

A Commission is never taken from the principal deposit of the client. Company paid commissions are generally aligned to the length of the term of the contract. Most top insurance carriers carry similar commission profiles for products of similar lengths and benefits.

We've been asked in the past and to be clear, our agency has expenses like any other business operation and these are gross revenues received on every client application that is issued. These revenues offset our regular operation expenses, marketing expenses and salaries like any other business. In other words, in our operation, paid salaries are not paid commissions, these are two different line items.

To give a few examples of commission schedules; a typical street level commission for a ten-year fixed index annuity is generally 6-7% commission depending on the age of the client, sometimes less based on age breaks. A typical street level commission for a five-year fixed index annuity generally pays between 4.0% to 5% depending on the age of the client.

Many 12 year, 14 year, 15 year contracts carry higher commissions and fail on the test of "best interest" to the client. As I have stated, they favor the company and are usually sold to enhance the commission of the agent or agency for no other reason, feel free to prove me wrong.

Fees, what kind of fees?

Not all annuities have fees. The fees associated inside some fixed index annuities could range from .10% to 1.50% for a variety of reasons; strategy enhancement charges, liquidity riders with up front premium deposit bonuses, lifetime income riders or health benefit enhancement riders to name a few.

It's important to know if you're being charged and what you're being charged for, in every case. Not all fees are bad fees. Some deposit bonuses exceed 22% with a modest .85% fee. That's a significant enhancement up front available for growth compounding. You have to weigh the benefits.

When it comes to strategy enhancement fees, I have never reviewed an annuity statement with outstanding results from enhanced fee based strategies versus the regular strategies and no fee. The fees will cut the performance opportunity over time and you will likely give back your gains in fees each year.

Most lifetime income annuities that yield the "top" monthly lifetime income charge a fee. Consider it a management fee for the "best of class" offer.

A few large annuity carriers offer free lifetime income riders in their annuities as a hybrid approach to growth and income.

These companies promote a 'Sizzly' big Income base bonuses, but buyers beware, that growth may not be there as expected later on... More on mechanics of the "free" lifetime income riders in a minute. Let me say this again... There is no free lunch. Actuarially speaking, you pay for what you get and the company has already priced the cost inside the offer.

Market Value Adjustments

A Market Value Adjustment (MVA) is a mechanism in some annuities that changes the payout amount when you surrender a contract early, based on shifts in interest rates since you bought the contract. Could be for or against you and should always be disclosed on the statement copy. Check the fine print, don't be surprised.

SECTION 2.

GROWTH & INCOME CALCULATIONS

Is this return Legit? Can you make money in an Annuity?

With the recent competitiveness in product design and marketing of annuities, it is oftentimes hard to believe the kinds of returns being generated can and do equal that of market driven portfolios. A lot has happened in the last ten years.

Companies are competing for market share amongst each other and more attention is being gained by market investors looking for safer paths to growth and income. You absolutely can put yourself in a situation to achieve double digit growth and lock that in annually.

Proper Expectations

In the past 4-8% annual return was a regular expectation for growth in a fixed index annuity. Now with indices linked to the Nasdaq, hybrid strategies and financial engineering, higher participation rates, it is highly possible to see regular double digit average returns over a ten year window. I'll discuss indices in a minute.

Forecasting

It is important to maintain a conservative forecast when reviewing illustrations. A ten year average is just that, an average. Not a return expectation for every year, but from the average of ten years. We just went through 2014 to 2024. We had a dog year in 2014, chaos in 2020 (COVID), a down market year in bonds and stocks in 2022 and two up years in 2023 and 2024. This is a pretty typical ten year window for performance, 2-3 down years or zero years with mostly years with some gains to good gains.

While January to December forecasts sound great on CNBC, that is not the reality for annuities. Returns are constructed by your issue date or anniversary statement date. Annually or bi-annually depending on the strategy applied in the annuity contract.

Market factors can truly affect your returns up to the day of your anniversary date to be clear. For example, Feb. 20, 2025 the market began to drop with the news of "Liberation Day" promoted by President Trump, the tariff right sizing on China and everywhere else in the world. Well, this shift spooked the market, the S&P 500 dropped 21% in a matter of 46 days, to a bottom on April 7, 2025.

If your anniversary date landed in February to April, not so good for most investors' annuity statements landing in that annual window. You didn't take a loss in a fixed index annuity but you more than likely will not see a gain in the 2026 statement. There are options to select strategies that can best overcome these short term volatility exposures, showing the importance of wise advice.

Impatience

One more consideration. Your account statements arrive annually with fixed annuities in general. (there is one company outlier which sends quarterly statements, but nothing changes on the performance) Just because you don't see gains in the first year is not necessarily a sign you need to make a change.

With sudden market shifts like 2025 (Feb. 20 - April 7) this volatility plays havoc on indices not set up for the stress. More on this in a minute. It might be you're in the wrong strategy, but a review would prove this out.

Indices & Crediting Strategies

Years ago there were as many as 32 different crediting strategies, that number has increased but to what I'm not aware. What I do know is you don't need that many to create an excellent returning annuity. Annual Point to Point cap, Annual Point to Point with Participation rate and Monthly cap are just a few of the most popular.

Different strategies designed specifically around specific indices and product lines. It's a long list of 70 indices which we track performance monthly. Many crediting methods have been proven and many have failed repeatedly. It still amazes me that some of these are even offered, monthly average is an example of one that consistently presents at the bottom and underperforms.

For the annuity owner, optimally, choose a strategy with no limits on growth. A Participation Rate approach, (Not a cap) with excellent participation rates on an index that you can look up any day... S&P 500 or Nasdaq 100. If that's not available, then point to point capped is the next best option.

There are named indices from every investment bank around. Most offer nothing new, a renamed basic index account for the S&P, Nasdaq or Russell index or a blended index across multiple asset classes (asset classes determined by the manager) and maybe a volatility buffer built in. These blended indices might deliver in an up market, but a volatile market like 2025, they likely failed.

Some of these indices have serious hype and agendas attached... for example the ESG (Environmental, Social and Governance) allocations were pitched with a green agenda (woke) and delivered terrible returns. A fail. (AI) driven indices, fail again.

These AI indices are, by design, algo driven and should pivot with volatility, but apparently not so much - with 2025 volatility being too much - and they also failed.

It can be complicated choosing what to watch and who to trust.

We track an index for gains, we use a crediting method for that index and gains are added to the account at the end of the period, simple enough right?

Financial engineers have managed to make this complicated. So much so, you don't know what your index is actually investing in - and you can't track any previous growth of said index to know if it ever would have or could have made a profit due to backtesting. Financial engineering is what got us in the mess in 2008.

These new indices use backtesting methodology, watch the language in the fine print on performance. I have yet to see an (AI) index deliver better returns than basic S&P and Nasdaq Point to Point strategies.

The Zig Zag moves in the Spring 2025 Liberation day window, took the managers to task and they ate it on trying to salvage returns. The clients on these indices were the victims. No positive returns through the rest of 2025.

Let me address another mixed term problem out there with the creators of annuity strategies and products. Let's hit the conversation about diversification.

In the context of investing, diversification is a "portfolio" management technique, spreading risk across different asset classes, generally non-correlated assets, with the idea that poor performance in one asset class will be offset by other better asset classes when it comes to MARKET DRIVEN PORTFOLIOS AT RISK.

Keep in mind Fixed Annuities have no market risk. They are not in the market. They track a market index or some hybrid index. The gains from said index are added to the annuity contract on the anniversary date, rinse and repeat.

Here's another industry problem. I continue to see prospective clients with statements and illustrations where advisors have recommended using overly blended annuity allocations... showing not one, but 2, 3, 4, 5 blended allocations inside the annuity as if you're managing equities. They. Are. Not.

Advisors are being pitched on webinars and by company analyst spokespeople that this is the best way to deliver yield to the client. They suggest the use of multiple blended indices in one annuity. Not true. I will say it's the best way to make sure the inside allocators get paid and to continue this mediocre practice.

We just witnessed blended indices failing in 2025 in a volatile market window, a true test of what they were designed for and yet they failed. So when you add a few more failed indices together, what do you get? More. Zero. Returns.

If using multiple blended indices in one annuity is so good, show me the money. I want receipts. I don't want backtested garbage, show me a statement proving 10% returns in the past year using this methodology consistently.

The goal here is to have the guaranteed fixed index bucket achieve a yield from the "tracking" of a linked index, i.e. the S&P 500 or the Nasdaq for example.

Real index market growth.

It is not that the bucket is directly invested in that index. It is tracking that growth from the safety position of a "guaranteed account", (which cannot take a loss), waiting for that growth credit to be added. Example; a 90% participation of the Nasdaq, for a one year period. If it did 10% for the year, you'd receive 9%, added to your account value.

Now, there is no guarantee that the index will perform year in and year out, but when it does, why dilute the earning potential? You will never have losses from the market.

What purpose does it make to water down growth in multiple blended underweight investments when the goal is to yield a return from the actual market index. Keep. It. Simple. This blended pitch is what agents around the country are falling for until they wise up that their client didn't get the return they wanted.

Take a look at Feb. 20th to April 6th, 2025. We had a market correction of 21% with the Presidential announcement of "Liberation Day" and new tariffs. Well the market loved that so much, it dropped very quickly.... until El Presidente came back and stated, well maybe it's not all that bad for China.

Hedge funds, money managers first went short, then got their heads ripped off and got caught in a reversal up and had to unwind positions and go long. Because these indices did NOT pivot at all, most annuity statements didn't show a positive return through 2025.

Company reps didn't talk about this though, did they? I asked the companies and got some garbage response about, "Well, they're not supposed to turn on a dime"... Wait, isn't that the point of the algorithm to begin with? This mixed messaging smells like 2008.

This little 21% drop, just drop-kicked the returns of all blended index annuities in the coming year statements for 2025-2026. Wait and see. The owners of these allocations will likely see a BIG FAT ZERO - again.

I have even heard the spokespeople recently suggest, "Oh now that these indexes are out of favor, it's a good time to invest back into them." Huh?

As if that is a reason to support the concept? Hogwash.

Oh wait, you're an analyst. Who do they represent… (the very largest investment bank in the US) with a vested interest in the bias of their opinion.

Overdiversification is not your friend, blended indices are likely not your friend. Stick with a proven path, keep it simple.

Back Testing, Fine Print, Illustrations

Back testing is and isn't a problem. Some of the indices are specialty names. For example Standard & Poor's has hundreds of versions. Some variations with % volatility buffers and some for branding. But not all are performers.

Also, when it comes to performance, Nasdaq has out performed S&P for 15 years, but all we tend to see offered in the past from annuity product creators was the S&P variety, hmmm (favored selling agreements). I like Nasdaq indices. You're carrying around Nasdaq tech in your pocket every day. The Nasdaq offerings lately have been some of the top performers available.

There's always fine print at the end in the disclosures, that's pretty much a given with this investment product space. Illustrations should be clear and straight forward and performance should be trackable.

Bottomline, these products do work if chosen properly and for the purpose and the client in mind.

Death by a 1000 Cuts, When does 1% cost you 21%

Most people have the perception that a 1% fee paid is just a small slice of the total investment pie.

Let's apply some real-world math to this and see how well this holds up and see how small of a cut we're talking about.

Let's begin with Bob. Bob works, saves and accumulates $200,000 over his life through age 65.

Bob, at the age 65, takes his $200,000 and makes an investment with an investment advisor.

To keep things simple, in this example we're going to assume he doesn't take any withdrawals. The account grows at a compounded 5% interest rate.

Because of the selections at the advisory firm made for Bob, he agrees to give them a small cut, a 1% fee to be paid annually on the account.

As Bob's account increases, so does his 1% fee. From age 65 through age 90, Bob earned $413,666 and paid $86,870 in fees on that growing account.

So, we need to reduce his growth by the amount of fees that he paid. His net gain was $326,796.

Let's take a look at that ratio. When we do that, we see that 21% of the growth went to fees to generate the growth.

21% went to the house, Bob got to keep 79% and this is just at a 1% fee exposure.

Bob didn't just lose 21% of his growth, he also lost the opportunity to earn money on the dollars he paid in fees.

Economists call this Lost Opportunity Cost. Each year you have the fees and then the amount those fees could have earned. In other words, The $86K Bob spent in fees, could have earned him an additional $63,605 had he not paid the fees.

Overall, Bob lost over $150,000 over a 1% fee!

After the 1% fee and the associated lost opportunity cost, Bob was left with $526,796.

Had Bob not agreed to a 1% fee, he could have had an account balance of $677,271 and personally benefited from the additional growth.

What type of fees are we talking about?

Advisor fees, expense ratios, transaction costs, deferred sales charges, retirement benefit riders, longevity riders, enhanced health riders, wrap fees, soft dollar costs, turnover rate, contract charges, redemption fees, deferred sales charges, market value adjustments... we could go on.

Be mindful of the fees. More on the impact of what over 1% in fees could look like in a few minutes.

SECTION 3.

BONUS ANNUITIES

All about bonuses

Bonus annuities have been around for several decades. The incentive given up front to move money from another investment source. An incentive just like a price reduction, $5,000 off the price of a new car, today and today only.

Bonus annuities add a bonus to your deposit, enhancing the starting value and enticing you to stay around plus it allows the process of annuity refinancing, relieving the customer from a net loss position in an under performing account.

Because of the frequency in the marketing of bonus annuities, this has conditioned some customers to think that is the "best" option available when that may not be the case at all. It could actually mean giving up tens of thousands of dollars in performance. Read on.

With regard to bonus annuities, there is always an internal cost for an external gain up front.

These bonus annuities should be applied to a specific situation though, not necessarily the first choice in a new account offering. We generally use these to fix a situation that needs correction, whether it's a poor performance issue or a market drop issue, trying to recover losses. A bonus annuity may not be the best offer in comparison to "non bonus" offers available.

For example... a 5 yr FIA may outperform a 10 yr FIA with a big bonus up front and an internal fee, simply due to the participation rates offered. But be careful, as I will cover, there is no free lunch. Actuaries have done the math setups on payouts and crediting strategies. Oftentimes, the non bonus annuities will outperform the up front bonus annuities.

What's a bonus cost you

The actuaries that price the breakeven point on bonus annuity offers will compensate for the dollar cost outlay upfront by reflecting it in the deviations in the cap rates or participation rates on crediting strategy offers in . They will recoup the bonus outlay paid up front over time by reduced participation rates or lower caps on bonus annuity products and sometimes they will include a small annual fee if the bonus is large.

Comparing a 5 year annuity to a 10 yr annuity with a bonus:

- As an example; A 5 yr. Fixed Index annuity with no fee or bonus using the same credit strategy, starting at $200,000 with an average return of 12.96% would yield an estimated account value of $327,758 at year 5 and $676,514 at year 10.

Compared to:

- A 10 yr. Fixed Index annuity with a large bonus 22.50% bonus and a .85 annual fee starting at $200,000 with an average return of 8.93% would yield an estimated account value of $331,139 at year 5 (a slight improvement) and $528,961 at year 10, (a $147,553 shortage compared to the 5 year contract)

  That's a pretty big difference, $147,553 in the first ten years. But don't stop there. What impact could this have in a longer window.

  What about 20 years? The five year annuity earns $2,311,947 versus the 10 year annuity earning $1,253,547. A large difference of $1,058,400 over 20 years.

  What about 30 years? The five year annuity earns $7,979,918 versus the 10 year annuity earning $2,993,412. A Giant difference of $4,986,50!

  Round up and call it $5 Million. That's some life changing money! But wait, there's more...

Take it one more step, what if we weren't just talking about a $200,000 deposit, but instead what if we're talking about a $2,000,000 deposit from the start?

The five year annuity would yield at 10 yrs = $ 6,767,139, at 20 yrs = $23,119,446 and at 30 yrs = $79,799,176.

The ten year annuity would yield at 10 yrs =$ 5,289,609, at 20 yrs = $12,535,473 and at 30 yrs = $29,934,116 .

The five year annuity would outperform by $1,477,530 at 10 yrs, by $10,583,973 at 20 yrs and by a staggering $49,865,060 at 30 yrs!

Why use a bonus

The best use of a bonus is to replace the business of a non producing annuity the client currently holds, which would cause them a significant surrender charge loss, if they were to exit the contract without remedy. The companies have approved the practice of allowing the bonus to offset the surrender charges and market value adjustment fees, putting the client whole and oftentimes in a net gain positive position with a new crediting strategy - creating a refinance of the annuity.

Whether it's the repair of an underwhelming performing contract, the switch from variable annuity with fees and losses to fixed index annuity without fees and without losses or some variation that improves with an income rider or takes one away, bonus annuities are vital to allow the client to maneuver with the changes in the retirement journey.

Proper placement rules

When it comes to bonus annuity applications, most insurance carriers will not accept new business replacement applications with current annuity contracts under the age of 2 years since issuance. Also, they are requiring some clear benefit of change to the client. An improved performance opportunity, a change in retirement goals, maybe a need for an income rider or a removal of an income rider, the need for better death benefits or the need for enhanced health care benefits, a change in estate or retirement planning goals, whatever the case.

A few larger companies will accept replacement applications with current surrender charges on the contract up to the new bonus limit if other conditions are met. For example if the current account carries a 14% surrender charge and the new annuity offers a 20% bonus to offset the surrender charge, in most cases, that would be an acceptable case.

Unfortunately, most insurers are still stuck using the old path rules, capping acceptable surrender values at 5-6% surrender charges on new business applications.

Competition will eventually turn this to favor consumers in the years ahead.

SECTION 4.

INCOME ANNUITIES

Income annuities play an important role in retirement planning for many retirees. The confidence that you've taken the step to have your everyday necessary monthly expenses income source covered - without question - offers a level of security to your future self and your family.

This decision I have found is also not dependent on what one's level of assets might be. I've never seen a muti-millinaire turn down a Social Security check and in the same vein, having all your monthly expense load covered solves some basic needs problems. Whether it's $2,000 a month or $20,000 per month, expenses are expenses.

Lifetime income products have morphed over the years and we use sophisticated software to instantly sort the top offers at the moment to deliver to our clients.

Whether the income need is immediate or in the future, the offers are today and can and do fluctuate with market, interest rate and geo political conditions influencing the competitive position of the top insurers.

This retirement niche is so competitive, most top offers tend to land on about 5 main top rated carriers when we make recommendations. However, the shiny object makers have clouded the space with hybrid products. Some with large sizzly bonuses.

It's very important to use an independent analysis of all available offers when reviewing income illustrations. Whether you're sorting for a monthly income need or a best income derived from a total deposit amount from the start.

4 key factors in your Income Annuity

When comparing fixed index annuities with lifetime income riders, 4 main factors are used to compete in offers. They are: Rollup Rate, Payout Rate, Income Base Bonus and Enhanced Benefits.

1. **Rollup Rate** - Refers to the annual interest earned on the Income Base Value each year the Income base is not activated for lifetime income. Every year this account is not initiated for a lifetime income payout, it earns a base stated interest rate on the income base value. This is the first competitive floating variable companies can use to jockey for top position.

2. **Payout Rate** - Is the rate used to determine the Income Base Payment calculation, i.e. Income Base Value (x) Payout Rate = Annual Income Payment for life. This is the second variable that companies can use and internally adjust and to get competitive with when offering income payments. Note that payout rates for Joint accounts will be reflected less than those of single payouts.

3. **Income Base Bonus** - An Income Base Bonus is an incentive to increase payment calculations and compete with other carriers. The bonus is applied to the Income Base Value and is only a deposit to that value. It is often overmarketed and falsely perceived to be some special bonus on account value, which it is not. It does not make the product a better income vehicle. All other factors in combination determine the most competitive income offers. It does lift the value of the Income Base Value which is ultimately used to calculate the payment. More on the big lifetime income bonus marketing machine below.

4. **Enhanced Benefits** - Relates to the Excess Income received if a client or spouse in an Individual or Joint annuity were to fall into a long term care type event which qualifies for this income payment. Oftentimes, it is two times the normal income payment or 1.5 times the normal income in a joint income payment. This is an excellent back up plan for Long Term Care type events when a clear need is present and additional income could help solve the need for licensed professional care to relieve the spouse. Most of the carriers with top offers, blend in enhanced benefits. Be mindful of those lifetime income offers that exclude enhanced health care benefits. Major carriers may exclude these enhanced benefits to compensate for a large income base bonus. Ultimately these tactics will also reveal they are not the top income offer available as well. As mentioned before, if a big bonus was offered, something was taken away and it may be the enhanced health benefits.

Shiny Bonuses

Several top carriers heavily market Up Front Income Base Bonus annuities... 20%, 30% even 40% income base bonuses. This has caused a lot of consumer confusion. These Up Front bonuses are not applied to the account accumulation value that can be taken out and spent. The bonuses are only applied to the lifetime income base values.

These have also been marketed to clients with the "assumption" these somehow are the "Top Income" offers due to these same bonuses being offered, when in fact they are likely not usually the best income offers available, by a wide difference.

These "Free" Lifetime Income Riders use a hybrid approach to appear to be a big benefit. As I have said before, there is no free lunch. If a bonus has been offered, something is being taken away in exchange.

Keep in mind, this bonus on the income rider only comes into play if the income rider is initiated for lifetime income. Where the bonus was given, the internal performance on growth has been throttled down to compensate.

When it comes to income illustrations comparisons, we use all available lifetime income products that meet our standards, in our search for best income solutions, whether they have bonuses or no bonuses.

Most of the time, the top - "best of class" income offers include an annual fee for the lifetime income product.

As I have said, an income bonus is only 1 of 4 factors to consider on an income annuity.

Oftentimes, I have seen clients stuck in an income annuity scenario with little to no desire for an income rider which they were sold, or it was ten years too early in the process.

In addition, they present to me their real case of concern, lack of returns when it comes to actual account performance.

WIth the actuaries pre-adjusting growth potential internally on these Free Bonus - Lifetime Income products, the results I have seen have been mediocre returns on both the growth side and the income payout side.

There are better income annuities products available, take caution in offers.

Income annuity alternatives

What are the alternatives for income in comparison to an income annuity?

Most Fixed Annuities offer annual free withdrawal amounts, from 7-10% free withdrawals annually and at no cost. The returns and the payouts are not guaranteed, but there may be no fee for the annuity contract as compared to an income annuity.

If a client has no absolute need for guaranteed income and if a client maintains a reasonable withdrawal percentage (4-6%) and earns an average return of let's say 8% or better, this could be an alternative to an income rider, not to mention the estimated savings of 1% in fees per year.

On the Securities Side of the World, we use Structured Notes and Structured Note Funds to drive monthly income into an account. This would be an investment solution.

These structured notes are debt securities linked to three market indices; generally S&P 500, Russell 1000 and the Nasdaq 100. The "flash notes" have a one year term and offer a fixed interest payout monthly.

As of this writing, the last offering in December paid 11.55% gross return before fees and the fund was yielding 9.15%. These notes also carry a 30% principal buffer of protection to downside market risk before any capital loss.

So, it's principal protected up to the first 30% of annual market losses. Not the same as guaranteed lifetime income, but a very good alternative.

SECTION 5.

VARIABLE ANNUITIES

Variable annuities are basically mutual funds wrapped in a tax deferred contract. They are market driven investments designed for tax deferred growth using different selling agreements with mutual fund companies and investment banks to distribute fund access to consumers for use as retirement growth and income vehicles.

Because of the nature of the market investments offered and the layers of administration in a variable annuity, there tends to be high fees associated with the variable annuity structure.

Variable Annuity Fees

Variable annuity fees can range between 3-4 % per year when you dig deep. These relate to the cost of insurance contract charge, internal management fees, turnover fees, expense ratios, riders for lifetime income, just to name a few.

Variable annuities are market exposed and offer no downside market protection in most cases. The risk is not as obvious as presented. With the internal fees being as high as 4% and market losses as a possibility in any given year, sequence of return risk can play a big role when it comes to variable annuities in retirement planning.

For example, In retirement, using client with an (IRA) at age 73, If you have variable annuity account carrying a minimum 3% internal fee combined with the need to satisfy the annual withdrawal for Required Minimum Distribution for IRA income, any additional losses from the market exposure could cause the client to experience a triple dip effect on their account; which could be very hard to rebound from in a prolonged market drawdown.

Variable annuities vs. Fee based Advisor Class, the 7 figure difference

When it comes to variable annuities and selling agreements, the sky is the limit. Variable annuities fees start to stack up; between selling agreement fees on each sub account, combined with mortality & expense fees, combined with riders and management fees, the totals can exceed 4% per year.

There is a little known secret that fee based RIA advisors use to combat the fees associated in what brokerage firms offer with variable annuities.

You probably have not heard of this option because it is not sold on a commission basis. This is only used by fee based RIA Advisors.

Consider the Fee Based Variable Annuity. A fee based managed portfolio of mutual funds or ETFs inside a low cost tax deferred wrapper.

It's unfortunate when a prospect brings me a statement with 4%+ internal fees. The long term savings in fees using a fee based variable annuity as an alternative can literally be as much as 7 figures in savings over twenty years.

Here's an example of a recently retired Colonel I reviewed in Virginia. His current Advisory firm was recommended by a group of associated military retirees in the Virginia area. When I dug deeper, it was clear this account offering was just another (Large Retail Named) brokerage variable annuity account, saddled with heavy fees.

Using our RIA fee based flat rate variable annuity,, we dramatically reduced annual fee exposure. See the details:

67 Year Old Client, Retired Colonel, Single

Current brokerage variable annuity value = $1,482,740
Estimated annual return = 10%

Fees on the current BIG NAME brokerage variable annuity account: Insurance Mortality & Expense Fee = 1.6%

> Rider and Other Fund Management Fees = 3.50%
> Advisor Fee = 1.50%
> TOTAL of all fees = $98,160.83

Fees on the new RIA fee based account: RIA Advisor Fee = .80%

> BIG NAME Brokerage
> Annual wrapper charge = $240
> TOTAL of all fees = $13,286.19

Annual Savings = $84,874.64

Estimated Compound Savings over the next 20 years = $2,098,801 Now that's life changing.

What could you do with an extra $84k a year compounded back in your account?

Well the annual growth estimation over 20 years came to an EXTRA $5,464,795 over 20 years.

SECTION 6.

MISCELLANEOUS

The Power of Zero

One of the most important things to remember is that with a fixed index annuity you are buying a guarantee, a guarantee your principal will never take a loss in the market. This is huge when we experience the next 2008 or worse. It will happen again. Cycles repeat. People have short memories and want to compare results often. Always remember the basis for this choice first and foremost is the guarantee of principal.

If they knew what was going to happen, why did they lose your money?

It's easy to get an opinion, turn on any news channel and a red ticker feed is running above or below the story, screaming the latest urgent crisis.

We have our fill of experts we can choose to follow. The problem is, they don't and won't have your vested interest when the tough calls need to be made.

I've seen this repeatedly, big names get quiet when the tough times hit. They often have or had agendas that didn't align with yours and you could lose you millions by taking their unpaid opinion.

What you don't know can hurt you

"But a man of understanding walks uprightly. Without consultation *and* wise advice, plans are frustrated, But with many counselors they are established and succeed." - Proverbs 15: 21-22(KJV). Seek wise counsel.

Prior advisor setups, failures or poor advice

Poor advice does not improve without changing the source. Expecting a change without changing the advisor is usually futile.

Complacency

Death by 1000 cuts can also describe complacency. Your comfort in the mediocre could cost you thousands. Taking the most minimal amount of effort to double check your portfolio is just being a wise steward.

Rollovers, TSP, how does that work?

401(k), 403(b), 457, TSP accounts that need to be rolled over to IRA accounts all generally use the same process to complete an ultimate IRA Rollover setup.

As advisors, we assist you in establishing your IRA Rollover accounts with a firm or insurance carrier in advance and then assist you with the transfer of that account from your plan administrator or the Thrift Savings Plan to fund the new annuity.

Transfers/1035's how does this process work best?

Transfers and 1035 exchanges are part of the application process - these are institution to institution transfers only, to maintain tax deferral.

Roth Conversions

There are several major insurance carriers that have come on the scene to compete for the customers' Roth IRA conversion needs. Generally, the Roth IRA conversion strategy goes like this; the IRA account can be moved to the new firm and subsequently, once in place, can be partially converted to the Roth IRA in a strategy of the clients choosing, a conversion of a dollar amount for a number of sequential years for example.

$200,000 IRA converted over 5 years at $40,000 per year into the Roth IRA.

The Roth account is linked to the former IRA account making it a smooth process.

Best of Class Ratings

With over 70 insurance carriers to choose from, we limit our product offerings to best of class standards and work with the top 30 carriers available. It is important to be mindful of insurance carriers credit ratings in a general sense.

I have heard some high flying lifetime income offers presented by insurance companies carrying less than A- ratings. While this is still considered an investment grade, it's the bottom of the list for some reason with A.M. Best in their ratings and there lies the question.

SECTION 7.

FIX MY ANNUITY - DO I HAVE A PROBLEM?

Here's a FIX MY ANNUITY™ question checklist to consider:

1. Have you ever looked at your annuity statement and wondered where all your gains went?
2. Does it frustrate you that your advisor never calls with better opportunities?
3. Would an extra $30,000 in your retirement account change things for you?
4. Do you find your current account performance underwhelming?
5. Do you feel stuck with your annuity and question whether it's a good fit now?
6. Do you feel you're paying too many fees inside your annuity?
7. Are you uncertain what you're paying in fees?
8. Do you want more income from your annuity but without penalties?

9. Would a better income plan and a backup plan for long term care change things for you?
10. Are you looking for more stable consistent returns?
11. Do you want to preserve and protect your investment principle?
12. Do you want better growth?
13. Do you want to lower or remove fees?
14. Are you looking for a bonus solution to solve your current annuity problem?
15. Do you want a guaranteed lifetime income or access to lifetime income?
16. Do you want to avoid market losses?
17. Do you want an annuity diagnostic completed?
18. Do you want to de-risk your portfolio?
19. Do you want income alternatives in a market portfolio?
20. Do you want to replace a bond portfolio with something guaranteed?
21. Do you want creditor protection as a business owner?
22. Do you want sophisticated allocations inside an annuity structure?
23. Do you want a Fiduciary reviewing your account?
24. Do you want to prevent "sequence of returns risk" with a buffering annuity account?

So now you've seen how this works.

You've seen that it's possible to add five figures or more to your retirement accounts through annuity refinancing.

You've seen that this is for people just like you—retirees between 55 and 80 with annuities that have been underperforming.

You've seen that you don't have to go through the painful, expensive journey I went through—because I've already done that work for you.

You've seen real client stories—Dan and Pauline, Calvin, Dr. Van Buren—people who were skeptical, people who felt stuck, people who had been burned before, and how their situations improved dramatically.

You understand it's not your fault if your annuity isn't performing well.

And you understand what makes my approach fundamentally different from the captive advisors most retirees have worked with.

So now the question is: What do you want to do about it?

You have two choices... So here's where we are.

You now understand that annuity refinancing is real. You understand that people just like you are adding $20,000, $30,000, $50,000, even $100,000 or more to their retirement accounts through this process.

You understand it's not your fault if your annuity has been underperforming.

And you understand what makes working with an independent advisor fundamentally different from working with a captive advisor who can only show you one company's products.

So now you have a choice to make.

Choice #1: You can try to do this on your own.

You can call your current advisor and ask if there are better options available. Of course, if they're captive to one company, they can't show you what else exists in the marketplace. And if they're earning fees on your current annuity, they have no incentive to help you move it.

You could also try to research this yourself. Spend hours—maybe weeks or months—trying to understand surrender schedules, bonus structures, allocation strategies, fee disclosures, and which of the 30+ carriers out there are making the best offers right now.

You could attempt to navigate the paperwork, the compliance requirements, and the transfer process on your own.

Is that possible? Sure. Anything's possible.

But here's what I know from 34 years of experience: Most people who try to do this on their own either give up because it's too complicated... or they make a decision based on incomplete information and end up in a product that's not much better than what they already have.

Or... Choice #2: You can work with me.

You can let me do what I've been doing for hundreds of clients for decades. You can let me analyze your current annuity, identify exactly what's holding it back, and show you the three best options available in the marketplace right now—from 30+ carriers—that could genuinely improve your situation.

You can get a clear comparison, understand exactly what you're paying in fees, see exactly what growth potential looks like, and make an informed decision with complete transparency.

And you can have all of that done in three weeks or less. Now, which path sounds better to you?

Here's what working with me gets you:

First, you save time. Instead of spending weeks or months trying to figure this out on your own, you get a complete analysis and your top three options in a matter of days.

Second, you get access. I have relationships with over 30 insurance carriers. I know which ones are making the most competitive offers *right now.* I know which products have the best historical performance. I know where the hidden fees are buried. That's knowledge you can't just Google—it takes decades of industry experience to develop.

Third, you get clarity. No jargon. No runaround. I'm going to show you in plain English what's happening with your account, what your options are, and what I recommend and why.

Fourth, you get results. Remember, I only move forward if I can improve your situation by at least $10,000. If I can't hit that threshold, I'll tell you to stay where you are. But 80% of the time, when someone qualifies, we find a way to add five figures or more to their account.

Now, let me be clear about something: I'm not going to tell you that you need me. You're a capable person. You've made good decisions your entire life. You've built a successful career. You've accumulated wealth.

But here's the question: Do you *want* to spend the next few months becoming an expert in annuity structures and carrier offerings?

Or would you rather let someone who's already done that work—someone who does this every single day—handle it for you so you can get back to enjoying your retirement?

Because here's what this is really about.

It's not just about the numbers—although an extra $20,000, $30,000, $50,000 in your account is significant.

It's about what that money *means* for your life.

Maybe it's two or four really nice trips anywhere in the world. Places you've always wanted to visit. Experiences you've been putting off. Isn't it time to elevate your lifestyle? When will it be time?

Maybe it's helping your grandchildren with a down payment on their first house. Just like Bob and Susan did—they took their annuity refinancing savings and helped their granddaughter buy her first home. In today's market with high interest rates and rising prices, that kind of help can be life-changing for young couples.

Maybe it's just peace of mind. Knowing that your money is working as hard for you as it possibly can. Knowing you're not leaving tens of thousands of dollars on the table. Knowing you made a smart decision as a good steward of your retirement funds.

And here's the really big one:

What if this isn't just a one-time gain? What if we can also reduce the fees you're paying on your investment portfolio by 2% or 3% annually?

On a million-dollar portfolio, that's $20,000 to $30,000 saved every *single year*. Over 10 years, that's $200,000 to $300,000. Over 20 years? We're talking about half a million dollars or more that stays in your pocket instead of going to fees.

That's legacy-building money. That's money that can change not just your retirement, but your children's lives and your grandchildren's futures.

So when I ask if you'd rather do this on your own or work with me, I'm really asking:

Would you rather spend months figuring this out yourself and maybe get it right... or would you rather have an expert handle it for you in three weeks and know you got it right?

The choice is yours.

And here's exactly what I'd like to offer you

TESTIMONIALS:

Now, don't just take my word for it. Here's what Dr. Juan Pasada wrote in his five-star review:

Dr. Juan Pasada - *"Grace and I met Mark over five years ago. Mark consolidated our various investment accounts to make them easily accessible upon my retirement. He worked with us to attain a retirement portfolio that suited our needs. I retired in June and I could not be more pleased with Mark's financial advice and support. Mark is always available to discuss and answer questions. He makes the drive from Dallas to Georgetown on a regular basis to meet with us and I find that highly valuable. I enthusiastically recommend Mark Stoecker to anyone who is looking for financial advice who really cares about you and your future."*

David U -*"I had a great experience working with Mark. He provided us with the investment portfolio that we needed and was forthright with his advice as a fiduciary and completed the transaction without pressure. I would use him again."*

Notice what David said: "without pressure." That's how I operate. I give you the information you need to make a smart decision, and then I let you decide.

And one more—Dale, who I've worked with for 20 years:

Dale & Janet Garriotte - "I met Mark close to 20 years ago shortly after retirement. Through the years, I've had a few changes to balance the investments. The most important thing is that the investments have made more than I've withdrawn. So Mark, thanks for choosing wise investments. We were able to live very comfortably and should for several years to come."

Twenty years. That's the kind of relationship I build.

WHY NOW

Now, here's something critical you need to understand about timing.

The offers I'm showing you today—the bonuses, the rates, the opportunities—they won't be here forever.

Here's why:

First, carrier offers are fluid. Insurance companies compete for market share by making aggressive offers. But those offers change based on market conditions, interest rate environments, and competitive pressure. We literally had changes happen from Friday to Monday just last weekend. Offers that were available on Friday were gone by Monday.

Second, interest rates affect everything. When interest rates are higher, carriers can offer better rates and bigger bonuses. When rates drop, so do the offers. Right now, we're in a window where some carriers are making extremely competitive offers to capture market share. But that window won't stay open indefinitely.

Third, the 2023 rule changes created this opportunity. Before 2023, the industry had much tighter restrictions on annuity replacements. When those rules opened up, carriers started competing aggressively with big bonuses—some as high as 20%. But if the industry decides to tighten those rules again, this opportunity shrinks.

I'm not saying this to create false urgency. I'm saying this because it's the reality of how this industry works.

The offer that's available to you today might not be available next month. The 15% bonus one carrier is offering right now might drop to 10% or disappear entirely.

Being complacent is not a strategy. It's a lost opportunity.

So here's the investment for this consultation: $125 for 30 minutes.

Now, I know what you might be thinking: "Mark, you're telling me you might find $20,000 or $30,000 or $50,000 in improvements to my account, and you're only charging $125?"

Yes.

Here's why: This consultation is not where I make my money. I make my money when—and only when—I help you transfer your annuity to a better solution and the carrier compensates me for bringing them your business.

The $125 is simply to make sure you're serious. It ensures that when we get on the call, you've already done the work of gathering your statements and you're ready to have a real conversation about improving your situation.

Think about it this way: If I can potentially save you $20,000, $30,000, $50,000 or more, isn't $125 to find out if that opportunity exists for you a pretty small investment?

Now, I do have limited availability. I only have 20 consultation slots available per week, So if this sounds like something you want to explore, here's what I need you to do:

Step 1: Schedule your Fix My Annuity Consultation Book a meeting on this link: **https://calendly.com/mark-106/discovery-call**

Step 2: You'll pay the $125 consultation fee and select a time that works for you on my calendar.

Step 3: You'll receive an email confirmation with instructions on what annuity statements to gather and send to me before our call.

Step 4: We'll meet on Zoom, I'll walk you through everything I found, and you'll make an informed decision about whether moving forward makes sense for you.

It's that simple.

Book a meeting on this link: **https://calendly.com/mark-106/discovery-call**

Here's a few more case studies recently:

Tuvinsky - Aaron & Cynthia, ages 73 and 73 are retired real estate brokers. Aaron & Cynthia had invested in Variable annuities and Brokerage accounts for 10 years using the same brokerage firm. The returns were ok, but nothing to get excited about, it seemed like they were "treading water" in Aaron's words. Cynthia was not pleased with the account value drops and wanted to see some swift action because she was more tuned into security on the account since she wanted to travel to Europe to see their children. After review of the accounts, We uncovered large internal fees dragging down any return, in addition to redundancy as well as high volatility and losses. After our analysis and presentation of top 3 Best of Class offers, we found $133,650 in savings back on their $607,500. Needless to say, the Tuvinskys were ecstatic with the result and moved forward on a new plan with safety and growth.

Morgan - Bill & Leslie were newly married. Bill was a widower and retired real estate developer and Leslie was a recent widow. Leslie had inherited her husband's annuity account which had no gains for 4 years. She wanted to start taking withdrawals but the performance was so low this made her nervous to draw anything. Bill was unhappy with such a big name company offering a "sizzly" bonus with nothing to back up the returns. After the analysis, we did find a similar pattern of inhouse underperforming accounts along with an income rider that was never to be used as it was pitched. The analysis offered 3 top of class offers and Leslie happily chose the "best of" with the features she needed to start receiving income. The net gains to Leslie this account, $108,600 on $975,000.

Honeig - Melvin & Julie, Melvin is a recently retired refinery line manager in Houston. He and Julie are both 69. Melivin came to me with two annuity accounts reflecting underperformance for over 5 yrs. After the analysis, we found a similar pattern with the underweight companies. These two companies offered large bonuses initially and now have limited growth potential due to reduced participation rates, sometimes a tactic with certain carriers. After our analysis, we presented three top offers, each slightly different. Melvin and Julie chose the best with immediate access to funds and a great growth picture. Bottom line, the accounts were improved with net gains of $113,683 on $763,000. They are very pleased with their results.

WHY YOU PERSONALLY NEED TO ACT NOW

Now, here's why the timing matters for you *personally.*

You're not getting any younger. And I don't mean that in a morbid way—I mean it in a practical way.

If you're in retirement, or close to it, you don't have time to waste.

Think about it: If you're 65 years old and you lose four years to an underperforming annuity—like Calvin did—that's four years you can never get back. Four years of growth you'll never recover. Four years closer to the time when you'll need that money for healthcare, for long-term care, for leaving a legacy.

The sequence of returns risk is real.

Remember what happened in 2008 and 2009? People took a hit in the market going down, and at the same time, they were taking withdrawals. Some never made it back to break-even. Some took five, six, seven years to recover. And in retirement, you don't have five to seven years to waste.

Your retirement has phases. Age 60 to 70 is different from 70 to 80. And 70 to 80 is different from 80 to 90. Your needs change. Your risk tolerance changes. Your income needs change.

And the longer you wait to optimize your accounts, the less time you have to benefit from compounding growth.

Can you afford to outrun your money? Most people can't.

So when I offer you these bonuses—these incentives to act now—it's not just about creating urgency for urgency's sake.

It's because every month you wait is a month you're not benefiting from better growth, lower fees, and a strategy that's actually aligned with your goals.

And in retirement, you can't afford to waste months.

So if you're serious about finding out whether you're leaving $20,000, $30,000,

$50,000 or more on the table with your current annuity, now is the time to act.

Now, before I give you the final call to action, I want to share something with you that I think will help you make this decision with confidence...

THE GOOD STEWARD

Before we wrap up, I want to share something with you that I think gets to the heart of why this decision matters.

There's a principle I've always believed in, and it's this: We're not just account holders. We're stewards.

You didn't just accumulate this retirement money for yourself. You accumulated it for your spouse, for your children, for your grandchildren. You

accumulated it so you wouldn't be a burden. You accumulated it so you could live with dignity and maybe leave something behind.

And being a good steward means you don't just *have* money—you manage it wisely. You keep a watchful eye on it. You make sure every dollar is working as hard as it possibly can.

There's a reason farmers check their fields regularly. There's a reason business owners review their financials monthly. There's a reason successful people don't just "set it and forget it."

Because neglect has a cost.

And when we're talking about tens of thousands—or even hundreds of thousands—of dollars that could be gained or lost by not being aware of an opportunity or a weakness in your plan then looking the other way isn't stewardship. It's negligence.

Let me ask you: Do you consider yourself a good steward of the money you've worked so hard to accumulate?

Then act like it.

THE ROCKING CHAIR TEST

Here's another way to think about this decision.

I want you to imagine yourself 10 years from now. You're sitting in a rocking chair, looking back on your retirement.rock

And you're asking yourself a question:

"Did I make the most of what I had? Or did I leave opportunities on the table because I was too busy, too hesitant, or too afraid to take action?"

Now, I can't tell you what the right answer is for you. Only you can decide that.

But here's what I know: Nobody ever regrets getting a second opinion. Nobody ever regrets doing their due diligence.

The only regrets I've seen in 34 years come from people who *didn't* act when they had the chance. People who look back and say, "I wish I'd known sooner. I wish I'd asked more questions. I wish I hadn't just trusted that everything was fine when my gut told me it wasn't."

So let me ask you: When you're sitting in that rocking chair 10 years from now, do you want to look back and say, "I'm glad I took the time to make sure my retirement was optimized"?

Or do you want to look back and say, "I wonder what would have happened if I'd taken that call with Mark"?

The choice is yours. But you have to make it now.

THE ANNUAL CHECKUP

Think about this:

You go to the doctor once a year for a checkup, right? Even when you feel fine. Even when nothing seems wrong.

Why? Because you're smart enough to know that some problems don't show symptoms until it's too late. And catching something early is a lot easier—and a lot less expensive—than waiting until it becomes a crisis.

Your retirement accounts deserve the same level of attention.

Just because your annuity statement shows up in the mail and nothing looks *obviously* wrong doesn't mean everything is optimized. It doesn't mean you're not paying hidden fees. It doesn't mean there aren't better options available now that weren't available when you first bought it.

Let me ask you: Do you go to the doctor for regular checkups even when you feel fine?

Then why wouldn't you do the same for your retirement accounts—especially when the potential upside is five figures or more?

This consultation is your financial checkup. It's your chance to make sure everything is working the way it should. And if it's not, we fix it before it becomes a bigger problem.

YOU DESERVE THE BEST

Here's the last thing I want to say to you:

You deserve the best.

You worked your entire career. You saved responsibly. You made sacrifices. You delayed gratification. You did everything right.

And it's not greedy to want the best return on your money. It's not selfish to want every dollar working in your favor. It's not unreasonable to expect transparency and honesty from the people managing your accounts.

You earned this money. You deserve to benefit from it fully.

And if there's a way to add $20,000, $30,000, $50,000 or more to your account—without taking on more risk, without changing your goals, just by repositioning into a better product—then you deserve to know about it.

So let me ask you one final question: Do you believe you deserve to have your retirement money working as hard for you as it possibly can?

Then give yourself permission to explore this opportunity.

APPROPRIATENESS FOR ME PERSONALLY

Look, I understand if you're still on the fence. This is a big decision. Your retirement money is important. You don't want to make a mistake.

But here's what I want you to understand:

Taking this consultation is not a commitment to change anything. It's a commitment to being informed. It's a commitment to being a good steward. It's a commitment to making sure you're not leaving money on the table.

And if I look at your situation and tell you that you're already in a great position and there's nothing we can do to improve it by at least $10,000, then you'll have peace of mind knowing you checked. You'll sleep better knowing you didn't miss an opportunity.

But if I *do* find $20,000, $30,000, $50,000 or more in potential improvements—and 80% of the time, I do—then this $125 consultation will be the best investment you made all year.

Here's the truth: The only inappropriate decision is the decision not to look.

Because if you don't look, you'll never know. And "what if" is a terrible way to spend your retirement.

So the question isn't "Is this right for me?"

The question is: "Am I willing to invest 30 minutes and $125 to find out if I'm leaving tens of thousands of dollars on the table?"

And if you're a good steward of your money—which I believe you are—the answer is yes.

So let me bring this all together for you one final time...

Alright, let me bring this all together for you and make sure you understand exactly what you're getting when you book your Fix My Annuity Consultation today.

Here's what you're receiving:

You're getting a one-on-one, 30-minute Zoom call with me personally—a Registered Investment Advisor with 34 years of experience, operating as an independent fiduciary across 48 states.

On that call, I'm going to:

- Analyze your current annuity situation with complete transparency
- Show you exactly what fees you're paying (both visible and hidden)

- Identify any riders or features you're paying for that don't align with your actual goals

- Present you with the top three alternatives available from my 30+ carrier relationships

- Give you a clear recommendation on which option is best for your specific situation

- Walk you through the entire process if you decide to move forward

And remember my guarantee: If I can't find at least $10,000 in potential improvement, I'll tell you to stay where you are.

Now, let's talk about the real value here.

The consultation fee is $125. But here's what we're really talking about:

If you're like 80% of the people I meet with, we're going to find somewhere between $10,000 and $100,000+ in potential improvements to your account.

Let's be conservative and say we find $20,000. That's a 160-to-1 return on your

$125 investment.

If we find $50,000? That's a 400-to-1 return.

And we've found as much as $136,000 for a single client.

But it's not just about the dollars—although the dollars matter.

It's about:

- Peace of mind knowing your money is positioned correctly
- Confidence that you're not leaving opportunities on the table
- Clarity about what you're actually paying in fees and what you're getting in return
- Legacy knowing you're maximizing what you can leave behind for your family

That's what this consultation really gives you.

And all of it starts with one simple decision: Are you willing to invest 30 minutes and $125 to find out what's possible?

If you are, then here's exactly what you need to do right now...

So here's where we are.

You've seen the proof. You've heard the stories. You understand how this works. You know what's possible.

And now you have a decision to make.

Here's what you need to understand about timing:

First: I only have 20 consultation slots available per week. Once those are gone, you're waiting until next week.

Second: Waiting too long can be a missed opportunity or a lost opportunity.

Third: The carrier offers I'm going to show you—the bonuses, the rates, the opportunities—they're changing constantly. We literally had offers change from Friday to Monday last week. The offer that's available today might be gone tomorrow. And you won't know what you missed.

So the question is simple: Do you want to be the person who acts while the opportunity is available? Or the person who waits and misses it?

Because I can tell you from 34 years of experience—the people who win in retirement are the ones who act decisively when the right opportunity presents itself.

By moving forward with the process, my clients are taking extra trips with family, they are helping grandchildren with their first home. They are changing their lives and they are elevating their lifestyle.

HOW TO TAKE ACTION

Here's what you need to do right now—and I mean right now, while you're still reading this:

Step 1: Go to https://calendly.com/mark-106/discovery-call

Step 2: You'll be taken to my calendar page. Select a day and time that works for you.

Step 3: Complete the payment of $125.

You'll enter your payment information to secure your spot. This is a small investment compared to the potential five-figure or six-figure improvements we might find.

Step 4: Check your email.

Immediately after booking, you'll receive a confirmation email with:

- Your scheduled date and time
- The Zoom link for our call = Instructions on which annuity statements to gather and send to me before the call
- A brief questionnaire so I can understand your goals before we meet

Step 5: Gather your annuity statements.

Before our call, send me your current annuity statements so I can do the full analysis. The more information you give me upfront, the more value I can provide on our call.

Step 6: Show up for the call.

We'll meet on Zoom at your scheduled time. I'll walk you through everything I found, answer all your questions, and show you your three best options. Then you'll make an informed decision about whether to move forward.

That's it. Six simple steps. The entire process from booking to having your analysis complete takes less than a week.

FINAL URGENCY PUSH

Now, I want to be really clear about something:

I'm not going to chase you. I'm not going to send you 47 follow-up emails. I'm not going to call you and pressure you.

This is your decision to make.

But here's what I know: If you don't take action right now—today, within the next 24 hours—one of three things will happen:

Option 1: Life gets in the way. You get busy. You forget. And six months from now, you're still wondering if your annuity is working as hard as it should be.

Option 2: The slots fill up. And when you finally decide to book, you've missed the extra value and you're waiting weeks to get on my calendar.

Option 3: The carrier offers change. The 22.50% bonus drops to 15%. The competitive offers disappear. And the opportunity you had today is gone.

Or... you take action right now. You book your consultation. And within 7 days, you have complete clarity about whether you're leaving $20,000, $30,000,

$50,000 or more on the table. Which option sounds better to you?

THE DECISIVE MOMENT

Look, you've already invested the time to read this book. You've already learned about annuity refinancing and how it works. You've already seen the proof that this is real and that people just like you are benefiting from it.

The hardest part is already done.

All that's left is to set the meeting on the calendar and take the next step. https://calendly.com/mark-106/discovery-call

So do it now. While the slots are still open. While the offers are still on the table.

Book your Fix My Annuity Consultation. And let's find out what's possible for you.

Now, before I let you go, I want to make sure you have everything you need.

If you have any questions about the consultation, about the process, about your specific situation, or about anything we covered today, here's how you can reach me:

Email my team at mark@onthemarkmoney.com

We typically respond within a few hours during business hours. My team can answer questions about scheduling, the consultation process, what documents you'll need, or any technical questions about how this works.

But here's what I want you to know: You don't need to have all your questions answered before you book. That's what the consultation is for. That's why we have 30 minutes together—so I can answer your specific questions about your specific situation.

So if you're sitting there thinking, "Well, I need to ask about X, Y, and Z first"—go ahead and book the call. We'll cover all of that when we meet.

Don't let a question stop you from taking action. Let the question be the reason you book the call.

FINAL REASSURANCE

I want to leave you with this:

I've been doing this for 34 years. I've worked with hundreds of clients across 48 states. I've helped people add five figures, six figures to their retirement accounts. I've seen what works and what doesn't.

And I can tell you with absolute confidence: Most people who take this consultation are glad they did.

Even the ones who end up staying in their current annuity—because at least they have peace of mind knowing they checked. At least they know they didn't miss an opportunity.

But the vast majority—80% of the people I meet with—we find significant improvements. And their only regret is that they didn't do this sooner.

So here's my promise to you:

I will treat your retirement money with the same care and respect I would treat my own. I will give you honest, transparent advice. I will show you all your options. And I will never pressure you into something that doesn't make sense for your situation.

You can trust me with this. Hundreds of clients have. And I won't let you down.

All you have to do is take the first step.

Book the Zoom call. And let's see what we can do together.

THANK YOU & CLOSE

Before I go, I just want to say thank you.

Thank you for your time. Thank you for taking your retirement seriously enough to invest this time to learn about something that could genuinely change your financial future.

That tells me you're the kind of person who doesn't just accept the status quo. You're the kind of person who asks questions, who seeks better solutions, who takes action when it makes sense.

And that's exactly the kind of person I love working with.

So I hope to see you on a consultation call very soon. I hope we find tens of thousands of dollars in improvements for you. And I hope that a few months from now, you look back on today and say, "I'm so glad I took action."

Remember: The slots are filling up. And the carrier offers won't wait for you. So don't wait. Book your consultation. And let's get started.

Take care. Be well. And I'll see you soon.